Allen's Authentication of Later Chinese Porcelain (1796 AD – 1999 AD)

Anthony John Allen

Allen's Authentication of Later Chinese Porcelain
(1796 AD – 1999 AD)

Anthony John Allen

Published by
Allen's Enterprises Ltd
PO Box 33-194
Takapuna, Auckland
New Zealand
Phone: +64 9 489 3135
allensantiques@clear.net.nz
www.allensantiquesnz.com

A catalogue record for this book is available from the National Library of New Zealand

ISBN: 978-0-473-25203-8

Printed by CreateSpace

ISBN 10: 1490568743
ISBN 13: 9781490568744

Book reformatted by Judith Sansweet:
www.ProofreadNZ.co.nz
PO Box 707 Orewa
Auckland New Zealand

COPYRIGHT © 2013

All rights reserved. No part of this publication may be reproduced, stored in a retrieval system, or transmitted in any form or by any means, electronic, mechanical, photocopying, recording, scanning, or otherwise, without the prior written permission of the publishers. Such permission, if granted, is subject to a fee depending on the nature of the use.

ALLEN'S AUTHENTICATION OF LATER CHINESE PORCELAIN

. . . continues on from the earlier *Allen's Introduction to Later Chinese Porcelain*, in a more detailed examination of aspects of dating; providing even the novice collector or dealer with information, dating techniques, and illustrations, which would otherwise take years to learn.

The focus of the work is primarily on the dating of porcelain made between the beginning of the Jiaqing reign in 1796 AD, and ending in the penultimate year of the 20th Century, 1999.

As many of the porcelains made in this 200-year period were copies of earlier periods, there are also a number of illustrations of genuine porcelain and pottery pieces made in the late Ming and earlier, Qing dynasties; i.e., prior to 1796 AD.

Progressing chronologically through the late Qing dynasty reigns of Jiaqing through Xuantong, this book then examines the porcelain of the Republic period (1912 to 1949), and then the Mao period of the People's Republic of China, before concluding with a preliminary look at the dating of Chinese redwares, and details of the author's visit to Jingdezhen in 1998.

With over 480 full-colour illustrations — not only of the items, but of their backs and undersides, close-ups of marks, footrims, and glazes — this is undoubtedly the most detailed English language text to date on the dating of Chinese porcelain of this period.

The author's often blunt and provocative commentary will undoubtedly offend some quarters of the Asian art world, but collectors for generations to come will thank him for his advice on detecting the bane of every collector's life — the Chinese porcelain fake made intentionally to deceive.

Also by the author

Allen's Introduction to Later Chinese Porcelain
Allen's Authentication of Ancient Chinese Ceramics
Allen's Authentication of Ancient Chinese Bronzes
Allen on Fraud

DEDICATION
To my dear wife, Elizabeth

COVER ILLUSTRATION

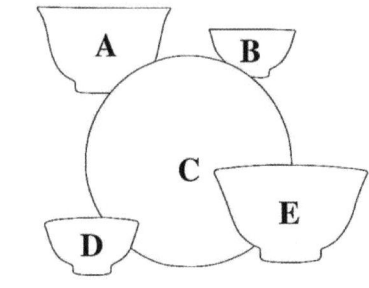

A	Guangxu mark and period	Fig 53.1(a)
B	Tongzhi mark and period	Fig 50.1(a)
C	Kangxi mark and period	Fig 7.1(c)
D	Guangxu mark but modern	Fig 50.1(b)
E	Guangxu mark but modern	Fig 53.1(b)

CONTENTS

PREFACE		
ERRATUM	"Allen's Introduction to Later Chinese Porcelain"	
INTRODUCTION		7
CHAPTER 1	Chinese Porcelain "A Brief Outline" 1500-1800	9
CHAPTER 2	Jiaqing Reign 1796-1820	43
CHAPTER 3	Daoguang Reign 1820-1850	53
CHAPTER 4	Xianfeng Reign 1850-1861	67
CHAPTER 5	Tongzhi Reign 1861-1875	73
CHAPTER 6	Guangxu Reign 1875-1908	89
CHAPTER 7	Xuantong Reign 1909-1912	135
CHAPTER 8	Republic Period 1912-1949	141
CHAPTER 9	Mao Period, Peoples Republic of China 1949-1976	167
CHAPTER 10	Post-Mao 20th Century 1976-1999	171
CHAPTER 11	A Preliminary Look at the Dating of Chinese Redwares (1700AD-1999AD)	177
CHAPTER 12	Addendum	219
CHAPTER 13	A Visit to Jingdezhen 1998	223
CHAPTER 14	Conclusion	231
TABLE 1	Principal Reign Marks of the Ming Dynasty	248
TABLE 2	Reign Marks of the Qing Dynasty	249
TABLE 3	A Selection of 19th and 20th Century Marks	250
SELECTED BIBLIOGRAPHY		251
GLOSSARY		255
INDEX		261

Editor's Note: For the convenience of the reader and in order to maintain consistency with the page numbers in both the Table of Contents and the Index from the earlier edition, no page numbers have been assigned to the front matter preceding page 7. This edition has 272 pages.

PREFACE

Three years have passed since the publication of "Allen's Introduction to Later Chinese Porcelain", and the response from my new-found friends and collectors around the world has encouraged me to attempt the formidable task of publishing a guide that will assist in the dating of most Chinese porcelains made after 1800.

One of the greatest difficulties I have experienced in attempting this project, as a non-Chinese speaker, has been accessing the wealth of recent Chinese research and archaeological discoveries, which have yet to be translated into English. The Chinese share a similar problem, for there appear to be very few Chinese experts who are familiar with the early Western writings, even by the great authorities Bushell and Hobson. I have also taken the opportunity, in writing this book, to blaze a trail in the dating of Chinese red glazed and underglazed red porcelains, and readers will need to forgive me if they do not share my fascination with this most misunderstood branch of the subject. Also of fascination to me is the matter of bubble definition, an aspect of dating which to my knowledge has never been discussed by earlier writers.

This book is not designed to supersede my earlier work but rather to complement it. I have endeavoured, with very few exceptions, to illustrate pieces which have not previously been published, accessing not only my own collection but also that of my good friend, Geoff Perkins. Obviously there has been some duplication, where for example I have expanded on the subject of "hollow lines", or glaze bubbles etc; and there are a number of pieces which I would have liked to have shown, but which were not available to me at the time.

I have approached the subject from a chronological viewpoint, where possible showing examples of reproductions, or pieces which may be confused with the originals, within the same chapter. This book is intended to be used as a guide only, for both the beginner and the advanced collector or dealer. I emphasize the word "guide", for the appearance of one or more features shown in this book will not necessarily by themselves prove conclusively that a piece is (or is not) of a definite age or period. I also stress the fact that my views, and datings, will not have universal acceptance, but if it subsequently transpires that I have made any material errors in this regard, then hopefully readers will find an "Erratum" in my next work; similar to that which is printed on the following pages.

If you are new to the fascinating world of Chinese porcelain, then I suggest you read "Allen's Introduction to Later Chinese Porcelain" first.

As with my earlier book, I have not "padded" this book with "auction catalogue-like" descriptions of each piece illustrated. In fact, I have deliberately abbreviated them to such an extent that I have no doubt that I will be criticised by some academic readers. Readers must look at the pieces illustrated and see for themselves the design or pattern. My interest is in the date of manufacture, not the historical background of a type or style of decoration (except if it assists with dating); information which may be gleaned from such excellent early works as C.A.S. Williams' "Outline of Chinese Symbolism & Art Motives". Nor have I stated, for example, "A six character Daoguang (1820-1850) seal mark in iron red enamels", but an abbreviated "Daoguang (1820-1850)". Readers are presumed to have learnt from my first book, the difference between seal and regular scripts.

ERRATUM
"Allen's Introduction to Later Chinese Porcelain"

Regrettably, since the publication of my first book in 1996, I have found or been alerted to several errors which I am duty-bound to correct.

1. The most serious error detected to date is my misdating of the lotus pattern saucer dish of *Fig 42(a)*, shown again here *(Fig 1.1(a))*. Mr Lei Rui Chun, deputy president of the Jingdezhen Museum, has confirmed it to be Kangxi mark and period (1662-1722). Coincidentally, I have since acquired an identical but restored saucer *(Fig 7.1(c))* with the calligraphy painted by the same hand, but not buckled as was the original one. This error in dating on my part has again highlighted the danger of relying on the Chinese written records, for clearly not all imperfect pieces made for the palace were destroyed; as a number of writers have stated.

Fig 1.1 Dating Corrections

Fig 1.1	(a)	(b)
Type:	Saucer Dish	Bowl
Design:	Lotus Pattern	Yellow Dragons on Blue Ground
Dimensions:	152mm diam	122mm diam
Mark:	Kangxi Six Character Underglaze Blue	Kangxi Six Character Underglaze Blue (Imperial Palace copy on inside footrim)
Dating:	Kangxi Period 1662-1722	Circa 1980

2. In *Fig 1.1(b)*, I have also again illustrated a bowl shown in my earlier book *(Fig 12(b))*, which I thought may have been made between 1930-1940. The consensus of several Hong Kong dealers, shown this bowl since publication, is that it is a museum copy made circa 1980, probably for the National Palace Museum in Taipei. As I acquired it in 1984 from the 'antique' shop in the Song Dynasty Village (Hong Kong), it must have still been 'warm from the kiln'.
3. The egg-shell thin brushpot shown in *Fig 68(a)* was initially dated by me as circa 1910-1915. For reasons which I will detail later (see *Fig 84*), my own research suggests that it is more likely to have been made between 1930 and 1940.
4. The Xuande (Hsuan Te) reign mark shown on page 88 differs from the mark found on excavated pieces from the Imperial kiln site, by the inclusion of the central horizontal stroke in the character *de* (top left). Genuine Imperial porcelain pieces do not appear to have this additional stroke, but I have been unable to ascertain whether or not this applies with non-Imperial reign-marked examples of the period. However, the appearance of this extra stroke is almost certain evidence of a later copy.

 Instead of

Genuine   *Fake*

5. On official (Imperial) Longqing (1567-1572) wares, the word *zao* appears in place of the word *zhi* (made).
6. Of the three hallmarks stated to be "Shendetang", two are not. While *Fig 39* reads Shendetang, *Fig 53(a)* reads Zengdetang, and *Fig 38* reads Jidetang. These marks may more properly be translated:

    Shendetang: Hall of discrete virtues
    Zengdetang: Hall of increasing virtues
    Jidetang: Hall of basic (fundamental) virtues.

    The traditional translation of Shendetang has been "Hall for the cultivation of virtue", but this appears to be a misinterpretation which has been perpetuated by a number of Western authors. I thank Dr Chiew of Singapore's Far East Gallery for drawing my attention to these translations.
7. "Sang de boeuf", or oxblood, should be spelled as I have typed it here, not "bouef".
8. The opening part of the sentence on page 138 disappeared behind the illustration of Fig 71. It should have read:

    "The jar of *Fig 71(a)* was purchased from a Hong Kong dealer, who from past experiences I had found to be honest and reliable."
9. On page 144, I stated: "I have never seen a yellow saucer dish of the Guangxu period with other than a black or brownish black mark". Immediately after publication, to my embarrassment, I found a pair with underglaze blue marks which I illustrate here in *Fig 61.1*.

INTRODUCTION

Possibly the most difficult decision to make in preparation for this book, was the title; for it had to reflect not only the period covered, but from a practical perspective, be short enough to be quickly written.

It was also apparent that even though I was restricting my writing to the period after 1800, if I was going to satisfactorily cover the fakes and reproductions made in these 200 years, then for less experienced collectors I would need to show for comparison, genuine pieces at least of the early Qing dynasty.

So, I have started with a few examples of Ming pottery and porcelain items, and progress through the early Qing reigns with a selection of what I consider to be fairly typical pieces, still available to the collector of modest means. My reason for showing these genuine Ming and early Qing porcelains is that many of them have been copied for perhaps 120 years, and it is sometimes possible to distinguish a genuine piece, say of the Kangxi period (1662-1722), with perhaps a copy made circa 1900; and both of them with a copy made say today.

The focus of the book, however, is on the dating of Chinese porcelain from after the reign of Jiaqing in 1796, and I have acquired and illustrated a number of representative pieces which I trust will be of interest and assistance to collectors, dealers, and academics alike.

For this book, partly from an economic viewpoint and partly because of the better close-up photographs, I have experimented with the relatively new technique of close-up digital photography. At times, we had up to six close-up lenses taped to the lens on the digital camera, and some of these relatively amateurish photographs have as a result, a very narrow depth of field; and blurring to the extremities. But, I have ended up with better definition than in any other book I have read on Chinese ceramics, and the majority of the photographs taken show clearly the features that I was emphasizing.

This book is not the final word on the subject of Chinese porcelain, nor is it intended to be. But hopefully, it provides the means to dating much of the later Chinese porcelains, and as with the aim of my first book, to restore confidence in the market place.

The overwhelming majority of people who have taken the time to write to me have been supportive of my objectives and in particular, I would like to acknowledge the following:

Messrs Geoff Perkins, Oliver Watson and Trevor Bayliss, in New Zealand for the loan of some of their collections, and to Geoff Perkins for the onerous task of proof reading.

Mr L H Tai, of Hop Wah Antiques in Hong Kong, for his friendship and assistance both in Hong Kong and in Jingdezhen. Also to Mr Chiang, of Chiang's Gallery in Hollywood Road, for his help in locating pieces which I sought to illustrate.

Mr Lei Rui Chun, vice-president of the Jingdezhen Museum, for his time freely given, in answering questions and showing me around Jingdezhen.

Mr Bill Hardy in Florida, USA, who kindly translated some of my more difficult texts.

Mr Burton Roberts in upstate New York, my newfound Internet friend, for his encouragement and support.

Denise Sowter for her typing and layout of the final draft.

And lastly again, my wife, Elizabeth, who has tolerated my at times eccentric passion for Chinese porcelain, and without whose help, this book would be just a dream.

Fig 2.2 Base View of Fig 2.1

Fig 2.3 Glaze of the Ming Period

Fig 2.4 Glaze on a Modern Fake

CHAPTER ONE
CHINESE PORCELAIN 1500-1800
"A Brief Outline"

In the 200 years since 1800AD, I doubt that there has been any type of earlier Chinese porcelain that the later potters have not attempted to duplicate. Certainly, the Song wares have been extensively copied, particularly the *qingbai* and the *langyao* ceramics, as have the Tang and Han figures and even the Neolithic pots. But, I had to start somewhere, and so I selected a few pieces from the later Ming dynasty (1368-1644), primarily to show novice collectors the difference between these and the later Qing wares.

1.1 Ming Dynasty 1368-1644

Fig 2.1   Genuine Ming vs fake
             (a)   (b)
Type: Figurine   Figurine
Design: Tomb Figure   Tomb Figure
Dimensions: 217mmH   187mmH
Mark: None   None
Dating: Ming (1368-1644) Circa 1997

The left hand figurine illustrated *(Fig 2.1)* is a genuine tomb figure from the Ming Dynasty, which would have been buried with the dead, and recently excavated. Even though it had a market value of only $HK500 in Hong Kong, these figures have been copied, as the right hand example evidences. The fake cost $HK60 ($US7) in the same shop.

Fig 2.1

The two pieces are remarkably similar, although close up inspection of the footrim and the glaze *(Fig 2.2, 2.3, 2.4)* show features which an expert will identify as modern. Particularly noticeable in this example, are the black flecks in the green glaze of the modern fake. Also to watch for is the dirt, which sometimes encrusts the genuine Ming figurines, and may be difficult to remove.

I mentioned in my first book the 'hot water' test and two Chinese dealers have since independently told me that if one licks the base, 'you can taste the age'. Personally, I wouldn't recommend this as if the item is a fake, chances are the piece may have been soaked in a sewer to artificially age it.

The little jarlet *(Fig 3.1)* is also of the Ming dynasty, and it shows the milky blue glaze, freehand drawing and hand carved foot so typical of the period. This jarlet is stoneware while the two figurines are of course earthenwares (pottery), rather than higher fired porcelain.

Fig 3.1   *Fig 3.2 Base of Ming Jarlet*

Type: Jarlet
Design: Freehand Underglaze Blue
Dimensions: 63mmH
Mark: None
Dating: Late Ming 16th Century

The eight blue and white dishes *(Fig 4.1)* are often referred to as Kitchen Ming, being made for the kitchens of the peasant population and sometimes for export to Indonesia and the Philippines. There is considerable variation in both the colour of the blue, which on some is almost grey, and the finish and decoration of the undersides.

Fig 4.1 Kitchen Ming Dishes

Type: Small Dishes
Design: As shown
Dimensions: 110-125mm diam
Mark: "Long Life" on one, "Upright" on another
Dating: 16th-17th Century

Fig 4.2 Reverse View

Fig 4.3 The central dish

Fig 4.4 Close up of bubble

Dishes of this shape continued to be popular into the 18th century, and readers may like to compare these examples with those later provincial wares of the Vung Tau cargo (circa 1690), auctioned by Christie's Amsterdam in April 1992.

I have shown *(Fig 4.3)* a larger shot of the central dish in order to show the beautiful milky glaze and depth of blue of much of the Ming blue and white. The close-up *(Fig 4.4)* was taken to illustrate this depth of colour, the blue disappearing in a mass of bubbles in the glaze.

Fig 5.1
Type: Bowl
Design: Floral scrolls and double happiness characters
Dimensions: 157mm diam.
Mark: None
Dating: Early 19th century (first quarter)

Fig 5.1 Kitchen Qing (Ching)

Bowls of the type illustrated *(Fig 5.1)* are often confused with the Ming. The Hong Kong Chinese dealer from whom I bought it, thought this bowl to be circa 1920, but to me it has the characteristics of pieces from the early 19th century; and in my opinion compares with the box later illustrated *(Fig 28.1)*. A similar bowl is illustrated in the Chinese publication, "Art of Folk Ceramics", (p 50), stating it to have come from Guangxi province in the south of China. Concealed among the scrolling foliage, one can see "double happiness" characters, cleverly mingled with the flowers.

The close-up photographs of the marks on two modern 'Ming' fakes *(Fig 6.1, 6.2 & 6.3)* are interesting because they also show the difference between two modern glazes. The first has large regular sized bubbles. Compare these two with the large and irregular bubbles of the genuine Ming saucer *(Fig 4.4)* and the difference is readily discernible.

Fig 6.1   (a)   (b)

	(a)	(b)
Type:	Tea Bowl	Tea Bowl
Design:	Underglaze red pomegranates	Underglaze blue & red figures
Dimensions:	83mm Diam	62mm Diam
Mark:	Zhengde Reign Mark (1506-1521)	Ruo Shen Zhen Cang (seemingly deep precious collection)
Dating:	Modern circa 1997	Modern circa 1997

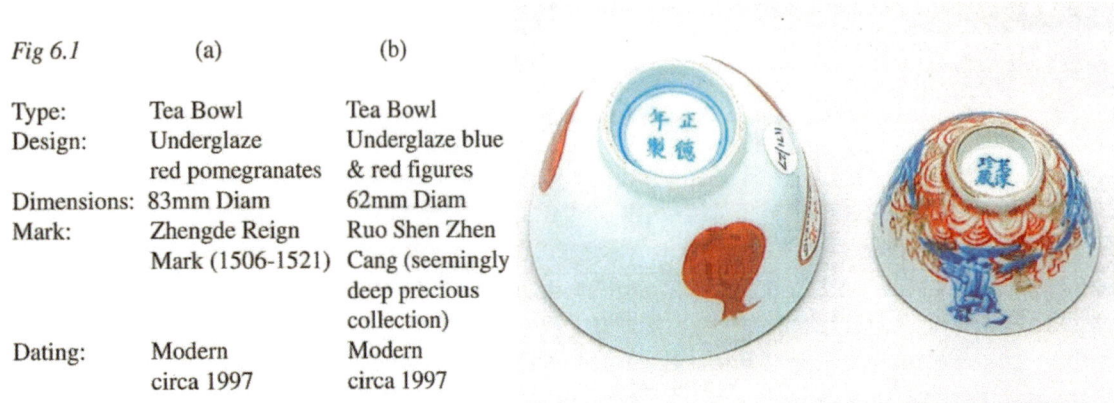

Fig 6.1 Modern copies of Ming porcelain

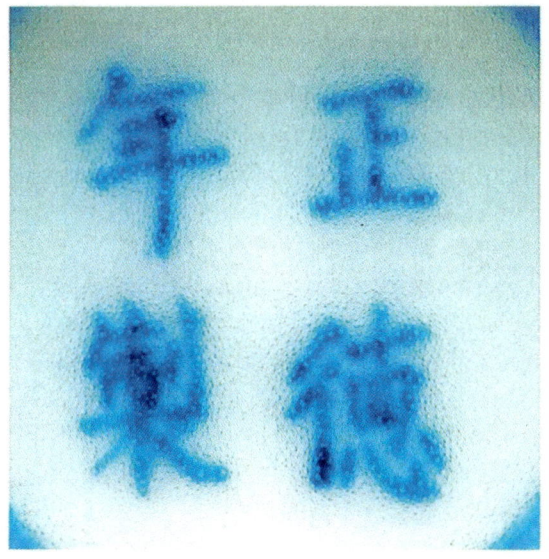

Fig 6.2 Close up of Mark (Fig 6.1(a))   *Fig 6.3 Close up of Mark (Fig 6.1(b))*

Also to be noted *(Fig 6.2)* is the relative consistency of the blue strokes. Compare this close up with say *Fig 7.3*, and the regularity of the strokes, so common to these modern copies, can often give a clue to dating. These strokes are unusually thin, while the purply blue *(Fig 6.3)* is a dead giveaway of a modern date; as of course is the absence of visible bubbles.

This has been the briefest of introductions to the ceramics of the Ming Dynasty, as I have not shown or discussed any of the Ming masterpieces; including the celadons, monochromes, enamels, nor the marvelous export pieces such as *kraak* or *swatow* wares. Interested readers will find a multitude of books on the subject.

1.2 Qing (Ch'ing) Dynasty
Shunzhi Period (1644-1661)

This reign was a period of great turmoil in China, owing to the warring factions in the southeast, which had yet to be suppressed and fighting would continue for 38 years. Porcelain of the late Ming (usually after 1620) to the end of this reign is commonly known as 'Transitional'.

It was a transition in design, in glazes, and in refinement; and a period which only until recently has attracted the attention of the fakester.

Reign marked or dated porcelain of the Shunzhi period is exceptionally rare, a fact which collectors should note in the event they ever come across it.

1.3 Kangxi Period (1662-1722)

By the early years of this reign, as is evidenced by a number of fine dated plates in major collections, the potters had mastered the art of not only underglaze blue, but also the elusive underglaze red.

The beautiful rich blue of the best pieces of this period is seen in the jar or vase (minus its lid) *(Fig 7.1(a))*. The technique of painting an outline, and then filling in the gaps with washes of blue, was a feature of the Kangxi period.

In *Fig 7.1(b)*, we see another example of this top quality porcelain. Note the application of the earlier apocryphal Chenghua (1465-1487) reign mark, possibly applied because of an Imperial edict not to use the reigning Kangxi emperor's mark. The Chenghua mark was being applied even in the last reigns of the Ming dynasty, as pieces recovered from the wreck of the Spanish galleon *Concepcion*, attest. Wrecked on a coral reef, 70 miles offshore from the Dominican Republic, in 1641, the recovery of the cargo was reported in the July 1996 issue of National Geographic.

Personally, I believe these earlier marks were applied, as they are today, solely with the intention to deceive. However, it has been suggested that following the ban on using the Imperial reign mark in 1677, the potters resorted again to applying apocryphal Ming marks. In addition, they sometimes simply left a double circle on the underside, or a sketch of an artemesia leaf, or the hare of the moon, twin fish, etc.

This bowl *(Fig 7.1(b))* has been treasured, and broken not only once and stapled, but broken a second time and re-stapled. Unfortunately, none of these three pieces have survived the last 300 years unscathed. Note how white this central bowl is in comparison with its neighbours.

The saucer *(Fig 7.1(c))*, as I stated earlier, is the pair to *Fig 1.1*, purchased by me four years apart in different parts of London.

Fig 7.1

	(a)	(b)	(c)
Type:	Elongated Jar (Vase?)	Bowl	Saucer
Design:	Landscape & Floral Panels	Lotus Scrolls	Lotus Scrolls
Dimensions:	170mmH	155mm Diam	152mm Diam
Mark:	Double circle	Chenghua (1465-1487)	Kangxi (1662-1722)
Dating:	Kangxi (1662-1722)	Kangxi (1662-1722)	Kangxi (1662-1722)

Fig 7.2 Footrim of Bowl (Fig 7.1(b))   Fig 7.3 Close up of mark on bowl

One of the common features of porcelains of the Kangxi reign, is the very fine levigation of the exposed bodies, as *Fig 7.2* illustrates. In later years, seldom was the levigation this fine.

The close up of the character *cheng*, on the central bowl *(Fig 7.4)*, illustrates the usual broad irregular strokes and fine bubbles, so common to the late 17th and early 18th century porcelains.

Fig 7.4 Enlarged close up of mark on bowl (Cheng character)

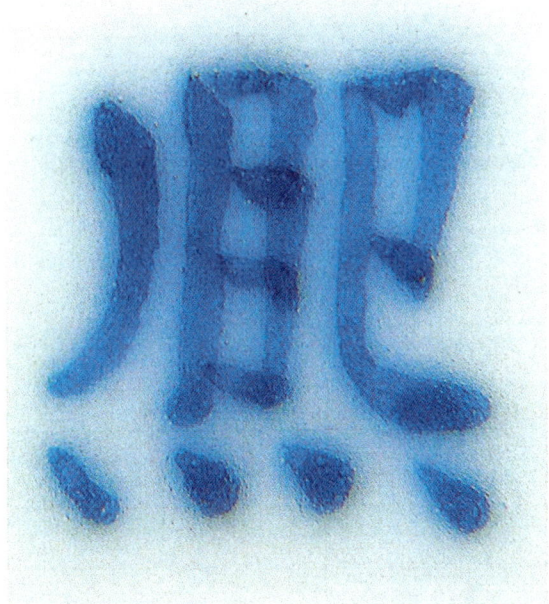

Fig 7.5 Close up of Xi character of Fig 7.1(c)   *Fig 7.6 Footrim of Fig 7.1(c)*

From the late 17th century, these beautiful porcelains became popular again in Europe, and in the 18th century particularly, the British and Continental upper classes had a fashion for ordering custom-decorated armorial services (see *Fig 134.1(a)*).

The plate of *Fig 8.1*, I believe dates to the first quarter of the 18th century. The large amount of decoration suggests a Kangxi period date, but I could not rule out the possibility that it was made a little later.

Fig 8.1

Type: Plate
Design: Floral
Dimensions: 275mm Diam
Mark: None
Dating: First quarter, 18th century
Collection: Geoffrey C Perkins

Fig 8.1 Export Plate (first quarter 18th century)

Fig 8.2 Reverse View

Unfortunately, porcelain did not necessarily change, just because the Emperor died, and many pieces must obviously bridge consecutive reigns.

In *Fig 8.3* is seen the usual iron orange footrim, and in this case, the potter's turning marks.

In *Fig 8.4,* again a close up of the underglaze blue and a point to note, for I have never seen this recurring feature on modern copies, a mass of little black spots embedded in the surface of the glaze. I say 'recurring' because unfortunately these black spots appear perhaps only in 10-15% of Kangxi period wares, sufficiently often to be a valuable confirmation of an early dating.

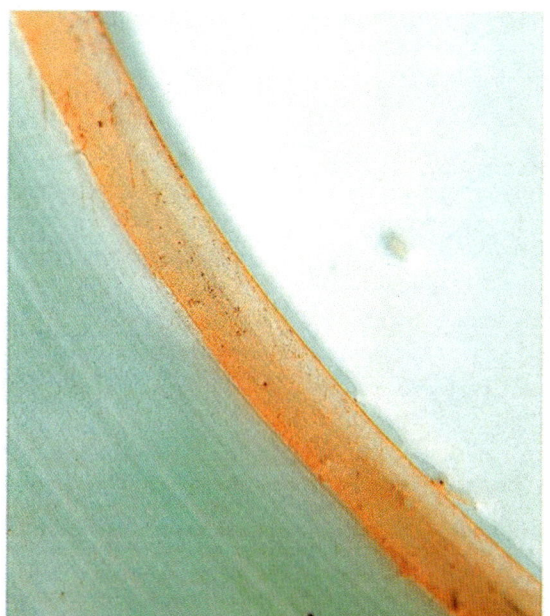

Fig 8.3 Close up of footrim

Fig 8.4 Close up of decoration

The recent recovery and auction of the Vung Tau cargo, which sank circa 1690, released large numbers of miniature vases on to the market, and while the little vases *(Fig 9.1)* were not in the auction, they may have originated from that source. I believe they date circa 1690-1710, except for the extreme right hand vase, which is later, probably circa 1780.

Fig 9.1 A Selection of Miniature Porcelain

Type: Miniature Vases
Design: Various
Dimensions: Vases 42mm-72mmH
Mark: None
Dating: All Kangxi period (1662-1722) except the right hand vase, circa 1780

In *Fig 9.2*, I have shown a close up of the footrims of one of the Kangxi miniature vases alongside that of the later right hand vase. Such comparisons are not always helpful, owing to the variety of finishes and firings.

Fig 9.2 Footrims

The porcelains of the Kangxi period have been much copied, and these three examples *(Fig 10.1)* are evidence of this. The left hand pale blue dish has provoked much discussion among the experts to whom it has been shown. This blue colour is more commonly associated with the early Republic period after 1912, but the reverse shows it, in my opinion, to be 19th Century, probably 3rd quarter.

The central saucer is of good quality closely approximating that of the Kangxi period and had it been inscribed with a Kangxi mark, it may have fooled the less experienced collector or dealer. Stupidly, the artist affixed a Guangxu mark (1875-1908), thus identifying it as modern, circa 1997.

The inkstone is also new, but bears a falsely dated inscription to the 5th year of Kangxi (1666), a timely warning to collectors who may believe that dated inscriptions have not been falsified.

Fig 10.1 Copies of Kangxi Porcelains

	(a)	(b)	(c)
Type:	Small Dish	Saucer	Ink Stone
Design:	Fish	Floral	Landscape Panels
Dimensions:	130mm Diam	130mm Diam	95mm W
Mark:	None	Guangxu (1875-1908)	5th Year Kangxi (1666)
Dating:	Probably 3rd Quarter 19th Century	Modern Circa 1997	Modern Circa 1997

Fig 10.2 Reverse View

19

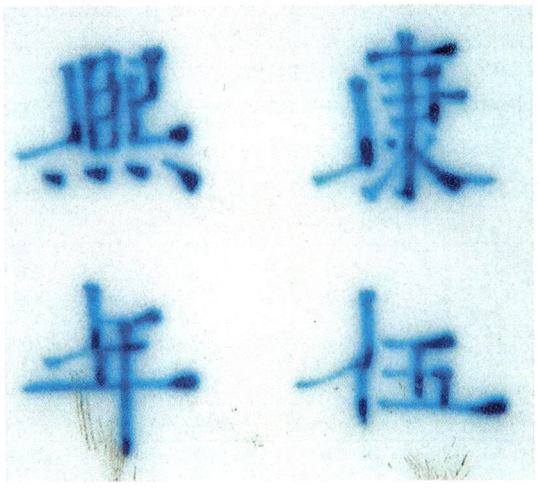
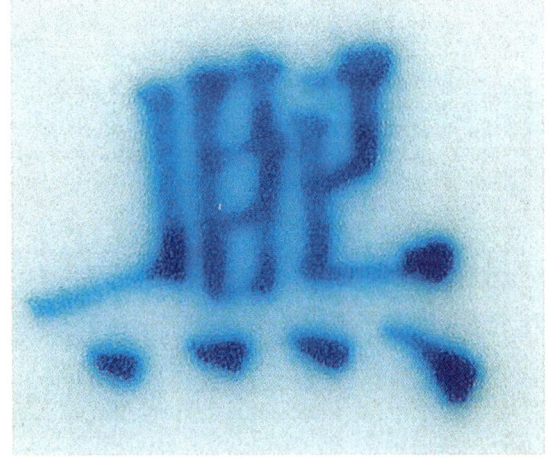

Fig 10.3 Close up of ink stone mark   *Fig 10.4 Extra close up*

In this instance, although the ink stone is modern, there is some irregularity in the colour of the blue, but the extreme close up *(Fig 10.4)* shows again the "icing sugar" bubbles of many of the modern forgeries. Readers should also particularly note the flatness of the modern glaze, which does not have the undulations and runs so typical of all of the Qing dynasty glazes.

The two yellow, green and aubergine saucers shown in *Fig 11.1* were purportedly made 150 to 200 years apart, the left hand one allegedly Kangxi (1662-1722), while its neighbour is Guangxu (1875-1908).

To quote Scherzer (see Tichane, p 191), writing circa 1882, *"And I believe that it would be difficult for the best expert to find the slightest difference between two pieces (both having for example yellow backgrounds and green dragons), one made 200 years ago and the other just out of the furnace, if six character indication of the reign did not come to his rescue"*. (Fig 11.1).

A design and colour combination which according to Chinese historical records was reserved for fifth rank concubines, the major difference between these two is the absence of the "ridge in the roundedness" (loach back) on the footrim of the Kangxi marked saucer, as can be seen by comparing *Fig 11.3 & 11.4*.

Fig 11.1 Saucers made for a Fifth Rank Concubine

Fig 11.2 Reverse View

	(a)	(b)
Type:	Saucer	Saucer
Design:	Green & aubergine dragons on yellow ground	Ditto
Dimensions:	132mm Diam	107mm Diam
Mark:	Kangxi (1662-1722)	Guangxu (1875-1908)
Dating:	Possibly Kangxi (see text)	Guangxu

I personally have misgivings about these allegedly Kangxi mark and period saucers, and at least one experienced Hong Kong dealer shares my views. If one compares the Kangxi mark *(Fig 11.2)* with say the known Imperial mark *(Fig 103.2)*, the former seems almost child-like. In fact, my Chinese dealer friend said it looked as though it had been written by a child.

Fig 11.3 Footrim of 11.1(a)

Fig 11.4 Footrim of 11.1(b)

The eminent Chinese porcelain expert, Hobson, writing circa 1915 (p 208) observed that in 1677 the potters of Jingdezhen were forbidden by an order of the district prefect to inscribe the period name of the Emperor. On the following page, Hobson stated *"and the Kangxi mark itself is comparatively rare except on the specimens which must belong to the later years of the reign"*. Why then is there today a relative abundance of Kangxi marked yellow, green and aubergine saucers, but to my knowledge, no unmarked Kangxi period examples? Perhaps these Kangxi marked saucers are later copies?

An interesting point that I have observed with all of these three coloured Imperial pieces in my collection is that regardless of which reign it is from, the mark is 180 degrees out of rotation with the design (ie: it is upside down when rotated).

The lidded vegetable dish *(Fig 12.1)* has been decorated with the enamel palette known as famille verte; green, blue, yellow, aubergine, iron red and turquoise (the latter colour absent here). Until the appearance of the foreign colours, or 'famille rose' palette, circa 1710, 'famille verte' had been the Chinese enamel palette since the Ming dynasty. The close up of the unglazed edge of the lid *(Fig 12.3)* shows the typical finely levigated body of the Kangxi period, while the enamels *(Fig 12.4)* with the exception of the iron red, are translucent; not opaque like many of the later enamels.

Fig 12.1 Famille verte decoration

Type:	Vegetable Dish
Design:	Floral Panels
Dimensions:	160mm Diam
Mark:	None
Dating:	Kangxi Period (1662-1722)

Fig 12.2 Reverse View

Fig 12.3 Unglazed edge of lid

Fig 12.4 Close up of enamels

Fig 13.1 Celadon glazed censer

Type:	Censer
Design:	Anhua (secret) Decoration under Celadon
Dimensions:	160mm Diam
Mark:	Kangxi (1662-1722)
Dating:	Probably Kangxi Period

Fig 13.2 The reverse

Fig 13.3 The footrim

The censer (incense burner) of *Fig 13.1* has given rise to a certain amount of discussion and dissent among the dealers who have seen it. Catalogued by Christie's as Kangxi mark and period (1662-1722), a dating with which I concur, it does not conform either in shape (see Geng Baochang, "Appraisal of Ming and Ching Porcelain", p198) or in mark, to most porcelains of the period. However, comparison of both the underside and foot *(Fig 13.2 & 13.3)* of this censer, with the earlier illustrated lidded vegetable dish *(Fig 12.1)* shows them to be almost identical. The grooved foot of this censer is a feature seemingly unique to the Kangxi period; although having said that, there is no guarantee that this groove has not been copied by a later potter.

The Kangxi period is also known for its 'Chinese Imari' porcelains *(Fig 134.1(a))* which were designed to compete with the Japanese Imari of the time. Chinese Imari was made in the period circa 1700 through 1745 and most pieces will date to these years. I have also seen two rare bowls in Chinese Imari, circa 1820 to 1850, made for the Straits Chinese market.

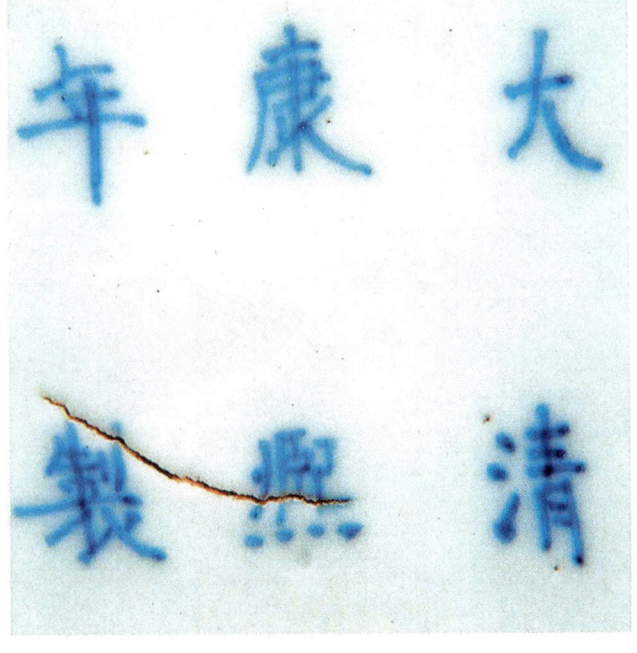

Fig 13.4 Kangxi reign mark

1.4 Yongzheng Period (1723-1735)

While the famille rose colours were introduced to China circa 1710, their use for most of the remainder of the Kangxi reign was largely restricted to the Imperial factory. By the following reign, these enamels of pink and white were available to the private kilns, and the Yongzheng period is known for the delicacy of the potting and decoration.

There are many books devoted to the Yongzheng porcelains and I refer readers to them. With the exception perhaps of the export wares of this period, and in the absence of a genuine reign mark, it is often difficult to ascribe a piece to the Yongzheng reign. Readers should note that many underglaze blue porcelains with a diamond shaped mark, the diamond in-filled with a cross-hatch and/or circle design, are ascribed by experienced Chinese dealers to this period. (See Qian Zhenzong and Xue Gui Sheng "An Appreciation of Qing Dynasty Porcelain", pp 379 & 380.)

Fig 14.1 Modern Day Copies of Yongzheng Porcelains

	(a)	(b)
Type:	Bowl	Saucer
Design:	Underglaze Red Bats under Celadon	Doucai (contending colours)
Dimensions:	165mm Diam	137mm Diam
Mark:	Yongzheng (1723-1735)	Yongzheng (1723-1735)
Dating:	Circa 1997	Circa 1997

Illustrated in *Fig 14 & 15* are three modern day copies bearing Yongzheng reign marks.

These two pieces are unmistakably modern, and readers will note the artificially dirtied footrim *(Fig 14.2(a))*, the excessive shine of the glaze (which is often subdued with acid treatment or sandblasting), and the too perfect glaze of the underside.

The saucer *(Fig 14.1(b))* has been decorated with the technique known as 'doucai', contending or dovetailing colours, and copies a known Imperial design of the Yongzheng period. (The overglaze enamels are dovetailed with the underglaze blue.)

However, the artist has carelessly omitted one bat; there should be five, not four.

Fig 14.2 The Reverse View

Fig 14.3 Footrim of 14.1(b)

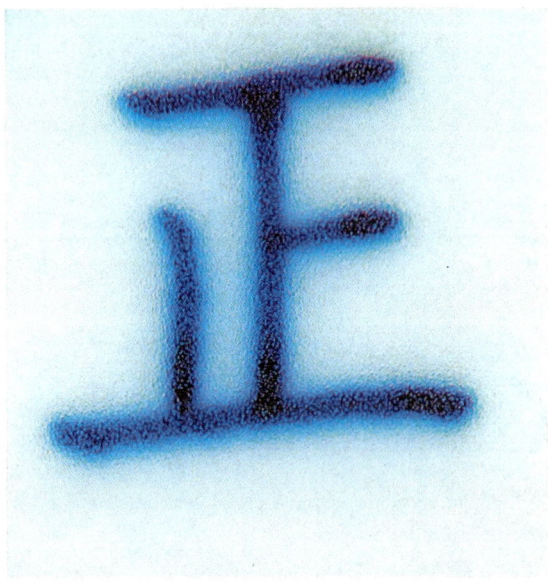

Fig 14.4 Close up of Mark 14.1(b)

The footrim illustrated *(Fig 14.3)* is remarkably well levigated, but the artificial dirtying combined with 'icing sugar' bubbles and regularity of the blue mark *(Fig 14.4)* are additional indications of a modern date of manufacture. I deliberately selected a 'doucai' piece to illustrate, as these wares were previously copied in the late Qing dynasty and early Republic. I will refer again to them later, but there are far too many 'doucai' porcelains, wrongly attributed to the Yongzheng period, usually with a Yongzheng reign mark, which often may be identified as copies (but are not) by a combination of 'hollow line' and the yellow footrim of *Fig 82.4*.

The decoration on the two bowls of *Fig 15.1* is absolutely exquisite and I have shown them here so readers are alerted to these top quality modern fakes. Note the shiny but matte appearance of the too perfect glazed underside, common to these and the previous two examples.

Fig 15.1 Modern Copies of Yongzheng Porcelain

Fig 15.1
Type: Pair of Wine Bowls
Design: Butterflies on a Yellow Ground
Dimensions: 90mm Diam
Mark: Yongzheng (1723-1735)
Dating: Circa 1998

Fig 16.1
Type: Underglaze Blue Plate (Export)
Design: Floral
Dimensions: 230mm Diam
Mark: None
Dating: Second quarter, 18th Century
Collection: Geoffrey C Perkins

Fig 16.1 18th Century Export Blue & White Plate

The broken plate *(Fig 16.1)* has the distinctive blue glaze which a number of dealers, myself included, associate with the Yongzheng reign. Made for export in the hundreds of thousands, plates of this type still survive in relatively large numbers. To allay criticism of a Yongzheng dating, I have shown it as second quarter of the 18th Century. Note the imperfections of the underside, the turned back foot *(Fig 16.2)* and most noticeable, the distinctly iron orange foot *(Fig 16.3)*.

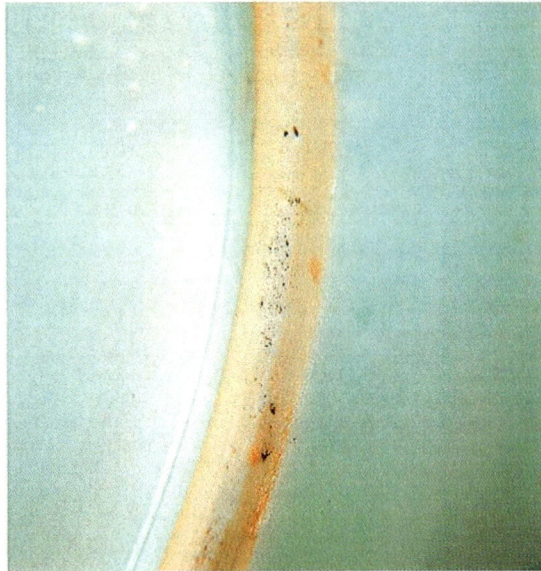

Fig 16.2 Reverse View

Fig 16.3 Close up of Footrim

The side view *(Fig 16.4)* shows the cobalt blue decoration has merged with the fired glaze. Note the very white body, probably indicating that kaolin from Mt Kaoling had been used. Kaolin from this source, according to Liu's translation of the Chinese historical records, was used also by the Imperial factory for two hundred years after circa 1600AD.

Fig 16.4 Side View

1.5 Qianlong Period (1736-1795)

The Chinese historical records, of dubious reliability, state that from the 11th day of the first month of 1735, private kilns were banned from using reign marks. By 1756, the ban was recorded as still operative, but it appears that by this date, 'seconds' of Imperial pieces could have been sold. These records would seem in this instance to be accurate, for the vast majority of Qianlong mark and period porcelains from private kilns, must date to the latter part of the reign (ie: late 18th Century).

In the second year of Qianlong (1737), the Imperial reign mark was standardised to that shown on the reverse of the plate *(Fig 17.3)*. There were exceptions to this rule, which I briefly discussed in my earlier book, but in the vast majority of cases, if the mark did not conform to this example, the piece was either from a private kiln, or a later reproduction. The close up of the characters shows that some strokes exhibit 'hollow line', but comparison with the close up of the 'classic' hollow line of the late Qing (see *Fig 62.4*) shows subtle variations. Also to be noted are the tiny bubbles which were often a feature of the early 18th Century, while the footrim *(Fig 17.4)* is beautifully levigated with a light yellowy ("straw") colour, smooth to the touch.

Fig 17.1 Qianlong

Fig 17.2 Reverse View

Type: Dish
Design: Stylised Characters
Dimensions: 200mm Diam
Mark: Qianlong (1736-1795)
Dating: Qianlong

Whether or not this dish is an Imperial piece, is a matter for debate, but when compared with the saucer of *Fig 18.1*, the difference in quality is immediately apparent.

Fig 17.3 Qianlong Mark (1736-1795)

Fig 17.4 Close up of Footrim

Fig 18.1 Comparison of Qianlong & Jiaqing Period Saucers

	(a)	(b)
Type:	Saucer	Saucer
Design:	Floral Scrolls	Floral Scrolls
Dimensions:	152mm Diam	152mm Diam
Mark:	Qianlong (1736-1795)	Jiaqing (1796-1820)
Dating:	Qianlong (1736-1795)	Jiaqing (1796-1820)

Fig 18.2 Reverse View

Fig 18.3 Close up of Qianlong Mark   *Fig 18.4 Close up of Jiaqing Mark*

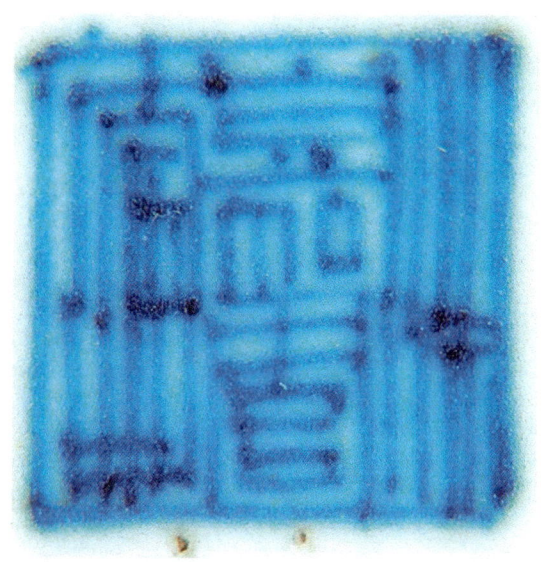

These saucers *(Fig 18.1)* are 'minyao', or people's ware, and must have come from a larger factory which as standard practice, almost invariably marked the reverse of this design with the reign of the ruling Emperor. The marks are crudely written, and the footrims do not show the same levigation as on the previous dish, while the typical glaze of the later period (1796-1820) shows the 'cracked or crushed ice' look of *Fig 18.4*

Fig 18.5 Footrim, Late 18th Century

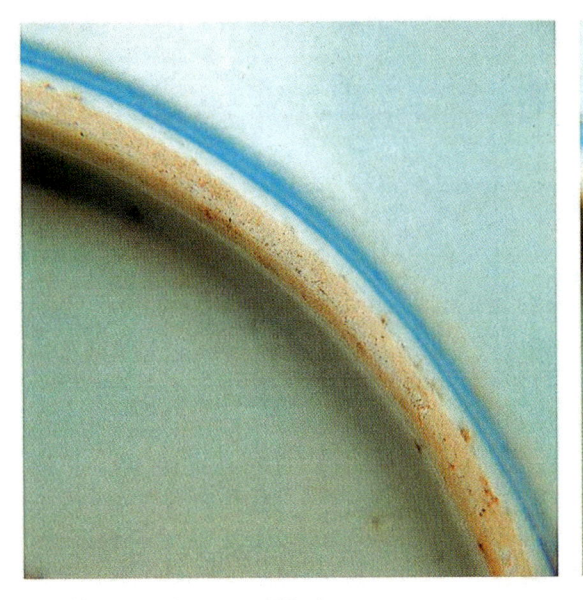

Fig 18.6 Footrim, Early 19th Century

Fig 19.1
Type: Sauce Dish
Design: Lotus Scrolls (Yin & Yang)
Dimensions: 96mm Diam
Mark: Qianlong (Four Character)
              (1736-1795)
Dating: Possibly Qianlong
              (1736-1795) (see text)

Fig 19.1 Qianlong Sauce Dish

Returning to the Qianlong period (or at least the Qianlong mark), the little sauce dish *(Fig 19.1)* has been cleverly sectionalised to show the Chinese Yin and Yang symbols. The blue colour in this instance is much darker, while the underside shows again the same yellowy straw foot of the earlier dish.

The Qianlong reign mark *(Fig 19.3)* has in this case been abridged to four characters, omitting the characters *da* (great) and Qing, a common occurrence on the smaller items.

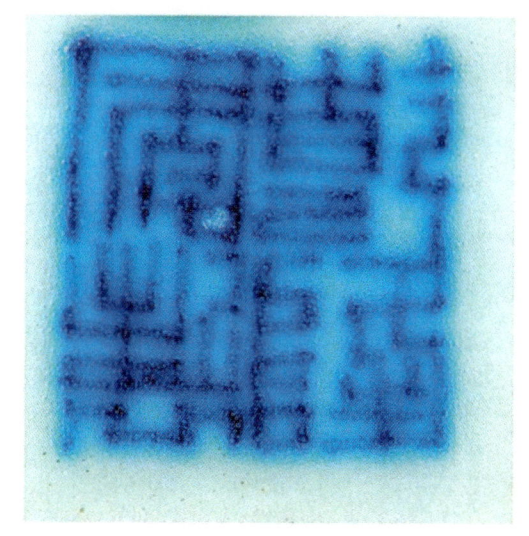

Fig 19.2 Reverse View　　　　　　　　　　*Fig 19.3 Close up of Qianlong mark*

It also has the 'reversed S' portion of the character Qian, which I discussed in my earlier book. This abridged mark was also repeated again on some late Qing and early Republic copies, so caution is necessary. The mass of bubbles shown in *Fig 19.3* is in my experience most unusual for glazes of the 18th Century, and despite the reassurances of several experienced Chinese dealers, I remain unconvinced that this sectionalised sauce dish is Qianlong mark and period. I strongly suspect that it was made in the early Republic, circa 1915-1930.

The two blue and white dishes, both with wide condiment rims *(Fig 20.1)* date to the early third quarter of the 18th Century, the dimpled corner example (b) probably postdating slightly the other.

Fig 20.1 Mid 18th Century Export Porcelains

	(a)	(b)
Type:	Octagonal Dish	Octagonal Dish
Design:	Trees in a garden	Shrubs by a lake
Dimensions:	270mm Diam	218 mm Diam
Mark:	None	None
Dating:	Circa 1750	Circa 1750-1765
Collection:	Geoffrey C Perkins	Geoffrey C Perkins

Fig 20.2 Reverse View

Fig 20.3 Footrim of 20.1(a) 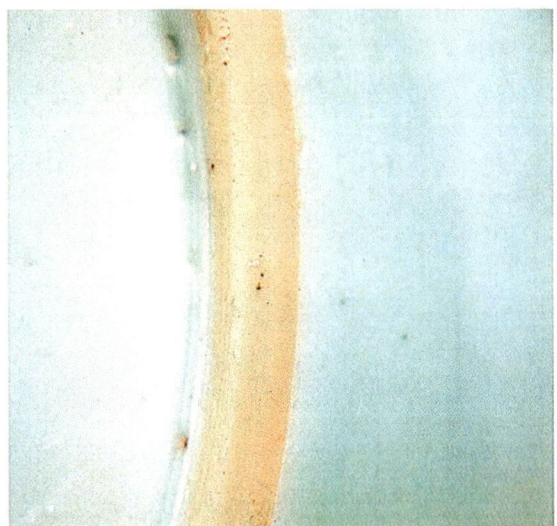   *Fig 20.4 Footrim of 20.1(b)*

Again, we see the orange footrims of so many of the 18th Century export porcelains. However, not all of the 18th Century porcelains show this orange foot, as the little tea bowl and saucer of *Fig 21.1(a)* reveals.

These two pieces *(Fig 21.1)* are examples of the top quality export porcelains available in the fourth quarter of the 18th Century. The teabowl and saucer were once part of a tea set, the damaged teapot otherwise identical except for the fact that its glaze had crazed in the manner of the 'soft paste' porcelains. Note the deathly white foot and grey (rather than blue) glaze of the underside *(Fig 21.2)*.

Fig 21.1 Late 18th Century Fine Quality Export

	(a)	(b)
Type:	Tea Bowl & Saucer	Reticulated Plate
Design:	Scrolls	Willow Pattern
Dimensions:	Saucer 120mm Diam	190mm Diam
Mark:	None	None
Dating:	Circa 1785	1785
Collection:		Geoffrey C Perkins

In my opinion, the enamel decoration of the tea bowl and saucer is not contemporary with the date of manufacture, the piece being embellished ('clobbered') at a later date, probably in England.

The central medallion of the saucer has been beautifully carved under the glaze, while the larger plate has a hand pierced design around the condiment lip.

Fig 21.2 Reverse View

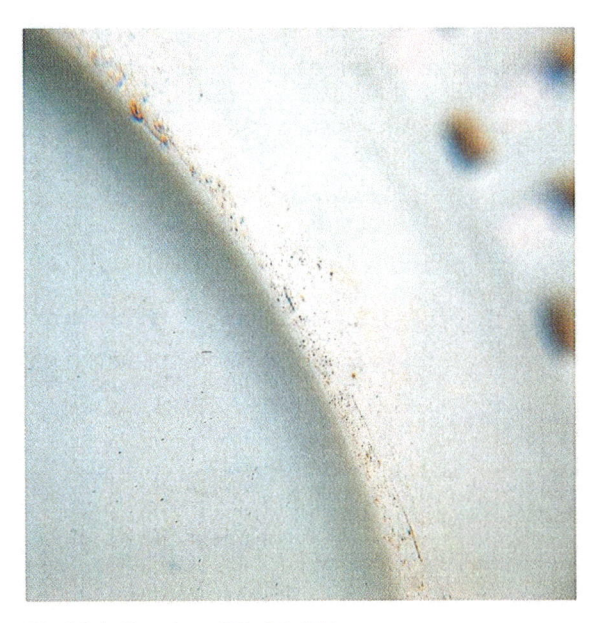

Fig 21.3 Footrim of Fig 21.1(b)

Fig 22.1 Spoons of the Qianlong Period

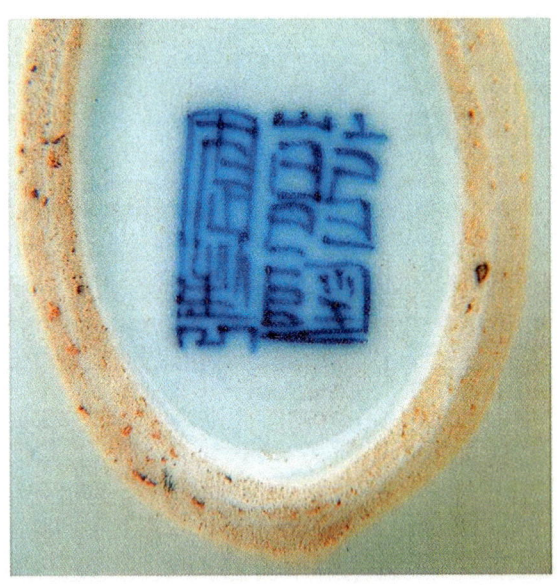

Fig 22.2 Close up of Footrim and Mark

Type: Spoons
Design: Doucai Scrolls
Dimensions: 125mm Long
Mark: 4 Character Qianlong (1736-1795)
Dating: Qianlong Period

This rare pair of spoons, in my opinion, dates to the latter part of the Qianlong reign, as the design and body have similarities with the saucer of *Fig 18.1*. Again, the four character 'reversed S' mark appears, carelessly written by an inexpert calligrapher. These photos also highlight the diversity of footrims and glazes found in the 18th Century.

Fig 23.1

Type: Bowl (Export)
Design: Figural Panels
Dimensions: 170mm D
Mark: None
Dating: Circa 1770

Fig 23.1 Export Bowl in Mandarin Pattern

Opinions will differ as to the dating of this bowl, as in my view it could be as early as 1765 and perhaps as late as 1780.

This mixture of underglaze blue borders, and orange with mauve figures, is commonly known as 'Mandarin' pattern, and was often used on garnitures of vases for the mantel piece.

Fig 23.2 Close up of Footrim

Fig 23.3 Close up of Enamels

Note the loss of translucency in the enamels, becoming more and more opaque as the years progress. The grey white glaze and white body on this export bowl, shared by the pieces of *Fig 21*, are distinctly different to the traditional blue tinged glaze with yellow (straw) foot, which the domestic pieces show. It seems probable that the export customers preferred a white porcelain.

Fig 24.1 Comparison of 18th & 19th Century Blue Glazes

	(a)	(b)
Type:	Small Bowl	Plate
Design:	Gilded Dragons on Blue Glaze	Gilded Dragon on Blue Glaze
Dimensions:	95mm Diam	190mm Diam
Mark:	Qianlong (1736-1795)	Daoguang (1820-1850)
Dating:	Qianlong	Daoguang

Compare also the beautiful blue glaze of the late 18th Century bowl *(Fig 24.1(a))* with the much inferior glaze of the later Daoguang period plate (1820-1850). Also note the blue tinged white glaze of the inside of the bowl has by the Daoguang reign, become a dull blue/grey *(Fig 24.2)*.

This dark blue glaze is often found on thick slab vases which have large lugs on the side, usually gilded decoration to the body, and frequently misdated to the 18th Century. Most are in my opinion, like this plate, early to mid 19th Century.

The gilding did not wear well, and as on this example, only traces of it remain.

Comparison of the close up of these two reign marks *(Fig 24.3 & 24.4)* perhaps 25 to 50 years apart, shows a distinct change in both the bubbles and the blue colour, as the quality of preparation and materials deteriorated into the 19th Century.

Fig 24.2 Reverse View

Fig 24.3 Qianlong reign mark of Fig 24.1(a)   *Fig 24.4 Daoguang reign mark of Fig 24.1(b)*

Fig 24.5 Footrim of Daoguang Plate

Fig 25.1 Qianlong Period Celadon Glazed Sherd

Type: Small Saucer (Sherd)
Design: Celadon Glaze
Dimensions: N/A
Mark: Four Character Qianlong
              (1736-1795)
Dating: Qianlong
Given to the author by Oliver Watson

Finally, in this briefest of introductions to porcelains before 1800, I have illustrated *(Fig 25.1)* a sherd of a small celadon-glazed saucer, mark and period of Qianlong (1736-1795), again, late in the period.

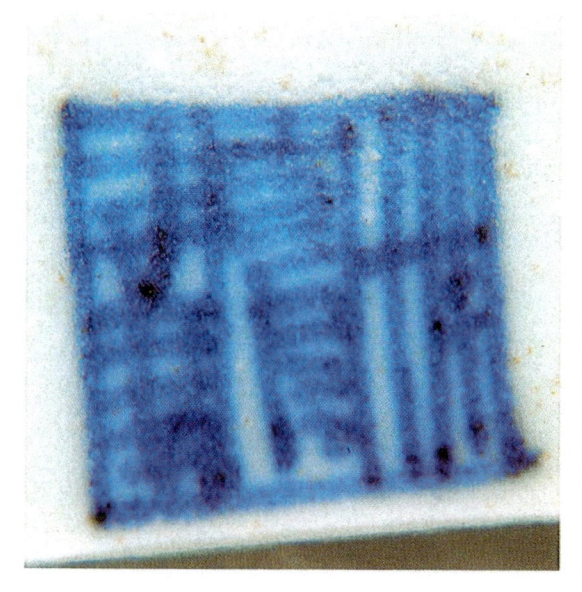

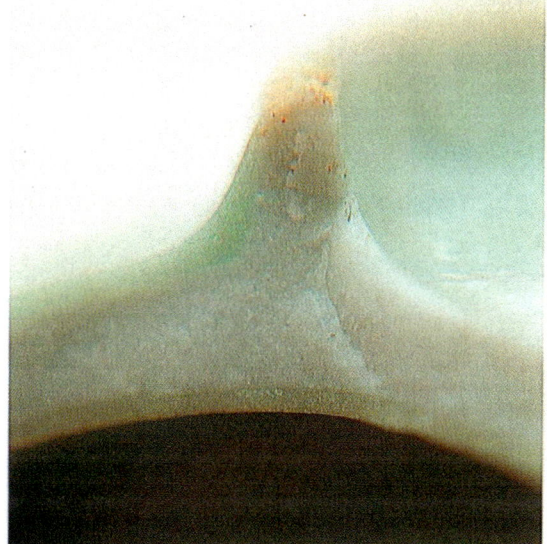

Fig 25.2 Qianlong Reign Mark

Fig 25.3 Cross-section

It is interesting to see the orange detritus clinging to the glaze (adjacent to the mark), much as the black spotting occurred on some of the Kangxi period wares. I suspect this was a firing defect, as my attempts at cleaning would not remove it.

The cross-section shows the usual white body, and note, the yellow (straw) foot emerges from the unglazed foot; not as some dealers think, from contact with the glaze.

I trust that these illustrations of late Ming and early Qing porcelains will prove helpful to both the novice and the more experienced dealers and collectors alike. Most old porcelains are unmarked, but if they do have a reign mark, more often than not it will be apocryphal. With the assistance of these close-ups, many 'problem' pieces should be positively dated; and hopefully museum curators around the world, will re-address some of their misdescriptions.

CHAPTER TWO
JIAQING REIGN
(1796-1820)

The primary focus of this book is on the Chinese porcelain of the last 200 years, and the Jiaqing reign makes a convenient starting point, commencing as it did in 1796.

The Qianlong Emperor had evidently abdicated and despite his senility, is generally believed to have continued to rule for the succeeding four years before his death. Perhaps this is the reason that so many snuff bottle collectors appear to believe that the Qianlong mark was applied in the Jiaqing reign, even as late as 1820.

While there is no certainty that some lone potter may have applied the Qianlong mark in the succeeding reign, the general consensus of the experienced dealers to whom I have spoken, is that the Qianlong mark was not applied (except in the Qianlong reign) before the reign of Tongzhi (1861-1875).

I mention this because several books on snuff bottles share this fundamental error, and one in particular is so hopelessly inaccurate in the dating of porcelain snuff bottles, that readers must question the reliability of what is otherwise an excellent visual reference source. This book, to which I refer, *"One Thousand Snuff Bottles"* was published in conjunction with an exhibition at the University Museum and Art Gallery, Hong Kong in 1993.

I have never seen so many errors in dating in a Chinese published text. Part of this collection subsequently appeared in a Sothebys London auction (24 September 1996). Presumably to save the embarrassment to the owner, the snuff bottles were not stated to be from this collection but buried anonymously under the heading "From a private Hong Kong collection". Sothebys did correct many of the dating errors from the exhibition catalogue, so interested readers who have this book should obtain Sothebys' catalogue for cross-reference.

I remind readers that they must read Chinese academic publications with some scepticism, for the standard of Hong Kong and Singaporean academic scholarship in relation to Qing ceramics (and later) is surprisingly poor.

Liu Liang-yu, quoting Chinese historical records, states that in early Jiaqing (presumably circa 1800), for a short period, the kaolin source in Official (Imperial) wares changed from Mt Kaoling to Ta-chou. Then from the Jiaqing to Tongzhi reigns, Hsing-tzu kaolin from Mt Lu was used. (Please note that I have quoted these authors verbatim and not attempted to correct their Wade-Giles (or other) transliteration to the *pinyin* used elsewhere in this book.) Liu then went on to say "Hsing-tzu kaolin has a comparatively low iron content and when mixed with potters clay gives rise to the extremely white body of official ware, although the texture of the clay itself is rather coarse ... except for a pale yellow streak where the biscuit meets the glaze."

These historical records are very unreliable, and the Chinese practice of generalising has been the cause of many errors in dating. Take, for example, the Imperial bowls of *Fig 32.1 & 35.2*, both from the Daoguang period. Neither piece has a coarse textured body, nor a yellow streak.

Fig 26.1 Minyao Porcelain from the Jiaqing Reign

	(a)	(b)
Type:	Saucer	Saucer
Design:	Lotus scrolls	Yellow sgraffito
Dimensions:	195mm Diam	152mm
Mark:	Jiaqing (1796-1820)	Jiaqing (1796-1820)
Dating:	Jiaqing	Jiaqing

Both the saucers of *Fig 26.1* are Jiaqing mark and period (1796-1820), with a bright orange foot that seems to be unique to the period. The colour change from a bluish glaze to the grey/blue colour of the early 19th Century is also apparent; as is the brownish rim on the yellow saucer. This brownish rim was probably applied to resist the 18th Century fritting problem, but it may also have assisted as a base to gilding.

Fig 26.2 Reverse View

Fig 26.3 Close-up of Footrim

Fig 26.4 Close-up of Enamels & Sgraffito Decoration

The close-up of the orange foot of the left-hand blue saucer *(Fig 26.3)* also shows the undulating glaze, while the close-up of the yellow enamel shows a very opaque red, yellow and green; and curious bubble-burst pinholes along the black/green borders.

Fig 26.5 Jiaqing Mark (Fig 26.1(a))

Fig 26.6 Jiaqing Mark (Fig 26.1(b))

Both close-ups of the reign marks *(Fig 26.5 & 26.6)* again show the 'cracked ice' bubble, variations in the density of the blue, and the glaze undulations, seldom seen on any modern copies.

Fig 27.1 Export Porcelains, First Quarter 19th Century   *Fig 27.2 Reverse View*

	(a)	(b)	(c)
Type:	Dish	Dish	Dish
Design:	Pekinese Dog/Om Character	Om Character	Starburst
Dimensions:	275mm diam	282mm diam	270mm diam
Mark:	None	Not translated (owners mark)	None
Dating:	First quarter 19th Century	First quarter 19th Century	First quarter 19th Century
Collection:	Allen	Geoffrey C Perkins	Geoffrey C Perkins

The three dishes illustrated *Fig 27.1* are typical of the export pieces made in the first quarter of the 19th Century. At least one private kiln had mastered the difficult technique of combining under-glaze red with underglaze blue. Two similar pekinese dog (or Buddhist lion dogs) dishes to *Fig 27.1(a)* were recovered from the 1816 wreck of the Diana, and auctioned by Christies, Lot 836 on 6 and 7 March 1995.

Dishes similar to *Fig 27.1(c)* have been found as sherds at the Wrightington Adobe Site, Old Town, San Diego (see Mudge, p 187).

The reverse *(Fig 27.2)* shows the filthy bases, common to many Chinese domestic wares, which I have partially cleaned to reveal the underlying unglazed body.

Fig 27.3 Footrim of Fig 27.1(a)   *Fig 27.4 Footrim of Fig 27.1(b)*

The footrims *(Fig 27.3, 27.4 & 27.5)* show the diversity of fired bodies in similar pieces of the period. There will undoubtedly be debate that some or all of these are in fact 18th Century, and while I cannot rule out that possibility, in my opinion the glaze colours and bodies suggest a 19th Century date of manufacture. The stylised Sanscrit 'Om' character (see on *Fig 27.1(a) & (b)*) was a popular design border, not solely reserved for the Southeast Asian market.

Note on two of the dishes the orange edge to the footrim, where the body meets the glaze, probably the yellow streak (on official wares) which Liu was referring to.

This iron orange edge is common to many of the underglaze blue porcelains of the first half of the 19th Century.

Fig 27.5 Footrim of Fig 27.1(c)

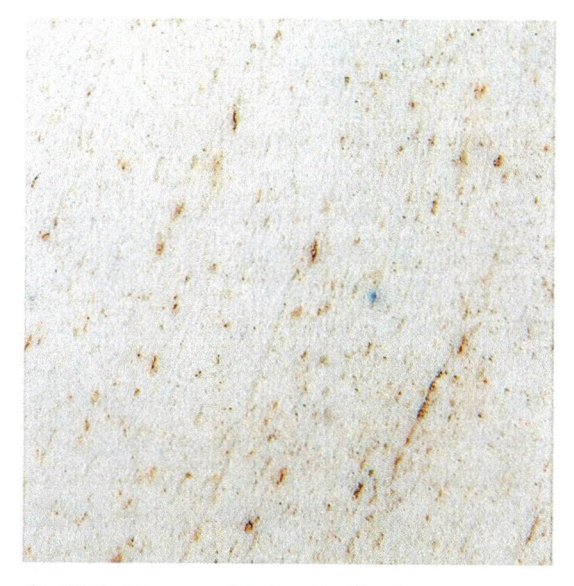

Fig 27.6 Close-up of Underside (Fig 27.1(c)) *Fig 27.7 Close-up of Underglaze Red*

The close-ups *(Fig 27.6 and 27.7)* of the cleaned body (of *Fig 27.1(c)*) and the underglaze red (of *Fig 27.1(a)*) show a mass of impurities in the body and an inky black blue, both possibly unique features of the early 19th Century.

If one just saw the low quality of these wares and the noticeable deterioration in quality in only a few years, it is understandable why the early authorities treated the period after 1800 with such disdain. But these were harsh years in China, with competition from British and Continental manufacturers, much internal unrest, and a little later, the Opium wars.

Fig 28.1 Porcelains of the First Quarter of the 19th Century

	(a)	(b)	(c)
Type:	Ink (Ashes) Box	Spoon	Censer
Design:	Floral	Islamic (Persian) Inscription	Landscape
Dimensions:	113mmL x 80mmW	120mmL	110mmD
Mark:	See text	Inscription dated 1815	None
Dating:	Circa 1810-1819	Circa 1815	First Quarter 19th Century

The lidded box *(Fig 28.1(a))* was I believe originally used to contain ink, but in the 19th Century, huge numbers were adapted for use as ash containers, for holding the burned bones of their ancestors. Shunned by today's Chinese because of the association with death, these inscribed boxes are to me a fascinating historical record of a person's life, for they have been inscribed with the historical details of the deceased. It is amazing to me that the Chinese government permits the sale of these important historical records; especially in a country where there is such a dearth of accurate details of any description in relation to life before say 1920, the Imperial family excepted.

I have briefly had the incised inscription on the inner lid and base translated. The deceased, name Lin, was born on 3 November 1735 (the last year of the Yongzheng reign) and died 22 June 1789, leaving three sons, two grandsons, and three great grandsons. On 6 December 1819 (Jiaqing 24th year), his ancestors burned his bones and this lidded box was probably bought new in that year.

Several Hong Kong dealers shown this box, including the vendor, are adamant that it dates to the Qianlong period (1736-1795); and one even suggested the neighbouring censer was Kangxi period (1662-1722).

It has taken me many years to appreciate how little some of these native Chinese dealers know of their own history, and at the risk of making yet another dating blunder, I have rejected their assessment.

The spoon *(Fig 28.1(b))* was made for export to Persia (now Iran) and bears a date AH1230 (AD 1815). The mark on the base is in the same coloured underglaze blue as is used on the box, and the distinct orange edge to the foot, reinforce my conviction as to their dating.

The censer however may even be a little later, being manufactured I think in the early years of the Daoguang reign, which commenced in 1820.

Fig 28.2 Reverse view

Fig 29.1 Modern Fake Bearing Jiaqing Mark
Type: Saucer
Design: Iron red stylised dragons
Dimensions: 154mm diam
Mark: Jiaqing (1796-1820)
Dating: Modern, circa 1997

Fig 29.2 Reverse View

Fig 29.3 Close-up of Modern Iron Red

Some of the modern fakes, such as the saucer *(Fig 29.1)*, continue to fool even experienced dealers and auctioneers. As I mentioned in my earlier book, collectors and dealers must learn to look for what is not there and the absence of imperfections in either the glaze or the iron red enamel should be a dead giveaway. Interested readers may like to compare this saucer with a pair of Yongzheng mark and period duplicates, illustrated *Plate 109, Qian & Xue's "An Appreciation of Qing Dynasty Porcelain"*.

The illustration of the two oval platters in *Fig 30.1* gives readers the opportunity to compare two modern fakes with the genuine export plates of *Fig 20.1*.

Note again the absence of imperfections in the glaze and the artificially dirtied footrim.

The smaller dish was sold to me as early 19th Century and because it has considerable genuine wear, I thought initially it might be. But it probably was used in a modern restaurant and in my view dates after 1990.

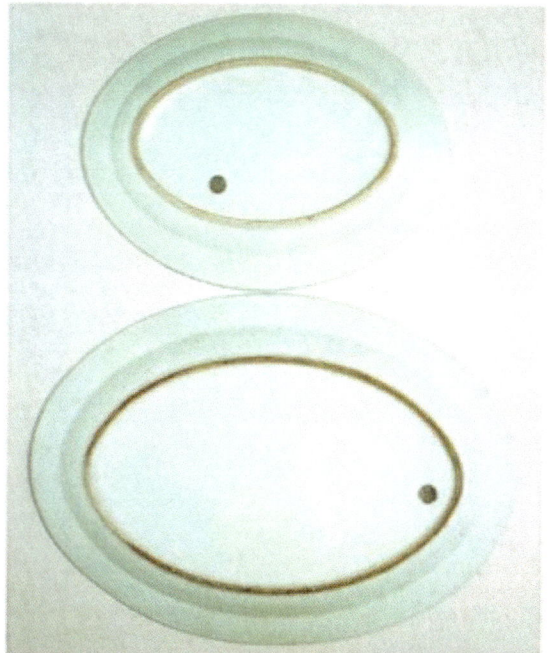

Fig 30.1 Modern Blue & White   *Fig 30.2 Reverse View*

	(a)	(b)
Type:	Oval Plate	Oval Plate
Design:	Nanking Pattern	Nanking Pattern
Dimensions:	303mmL x 225mmW	400mmL x 280W
Mark:	None	None
Dating:	Modern, after 1990	Modern, circa 1997-

Reign marked porcelain of the Jiaqing period, if made for the Imperial palace, is usually of very high quality and is becoming increasingly scarce, and expensive. The general decline in quality had started at the end of the 18th Century and it was really not for another 100 years before the quality improved again. However, there were some exceptional pieces made during this period of decline, but they are the exception, and in my opinion do not yet carry the rarity value which, were they say English porcelain, they would otherwise deserve.

CHAPTER THREE
DAOGUANG REIGN
(1820-1850)

There is considerable misunderstanding particularly among Chinese dealers, as to the dating of porcelains from this period. Some of these misunderstandings originate from a Chinese reliance on their hopelessly unreliable historical records. Liu, for example (page 35), quoting these records, states:

> "The so-called kaolin used by all the kilns at Jingdezhen for the manufacture of porcelain, consists of white clay extracted from Mt Lu." I stress the words "all kilns".

Ebelman & Salvetat (see Tichane, p 435), however, said:

> "The material sent by Father Ly contained two kinds of crude kaolin ... (p 437). We have not examined any other kaolins among the materials that the Chinese consider to be the 'bones of the porcelain'."

Not only does this imply that there were more than two types of kaolin available, of the two studied, they said (p 435, Kaolin from Tong-Kang):

> "The clay is very white and smooth to the touch ... It is still white and infusible after going through the high fire of a porcelain furnace."

(P 437, Kaolin from Sy-Kang):

> "The washed kaolin from Sy-Kang after treatment in the high fire, gives a yellowish product. The crude kaolin melts for the most part, and is full of specks of iron owing to the brown mica that it contains."

Now admittedly, Liu is quoting from records circa 1839 and Ebelman & Salvetat from circa 1844, and I suppose it is conceivable that at one particular period, only one source was available. But, it is irresponsible to say the least to quote one source, and knowing that it was demonstrably wrong, to mislead readers into thinking that only one type of body applied to the whole reign period. As readers will see from the pieces which I illustrate, the only consistent point about these footrims, is their inconsistency. I have little doubt that some readers will take me to task about my earlier comments that the Qianlong mark was probably not used before the reign of Tongzhi (1861-1875), and certainly the authors of the Chinese publication *"An Appreciation of Qing Dynasty Porcelain"* do not share my views; for on page 321 they illustrate such a piece. Even from the photograph it is possible to see that their four legged censer is not Daoguang period, but has the unmistakable blue of the Republic. This is not to denigrate an otherwise excellent book which although totally in Chinese, I still recommend to readers as one of the best visual reference sources available.

It is extremely rare to find blue and white porcelain of the Daoguang period from a non-Imperial kiln, with the contemporary reign mark. The 'cracked ice' or 'hawthorn' design was very popular in the Kangxi period (1662-1722), especially on ginger jars, and this piece *(Fig 31.1)* was probably commissioned by a wealthy member of the Chinese aristocracy. The glaze has been very thickly applied, with the runs visible clearly in the illustration *(Fig 31.2)*. This thick glaze with undulations is often known as "orange peel".

In *Fig 31.3 & 31.4*, I have shown two perspectives of the footrim, one from the side, one from above. This must surely be the 'Sy-Kang' kaolin which Ebelman & Salvetat were referring to.

Fig 31.1 Daoguang Mark and Period Charger (1820-1850)

Type: Charger
Design: Hawthorn
Dimensions: 415mm diam
Mark: Daoguang
             (1820-1850)
Dating: Daoguang

Fig 31.2 Reverse View

54

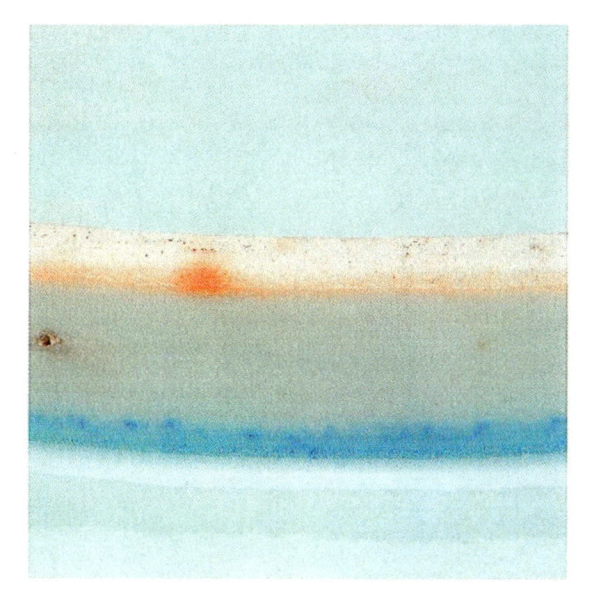

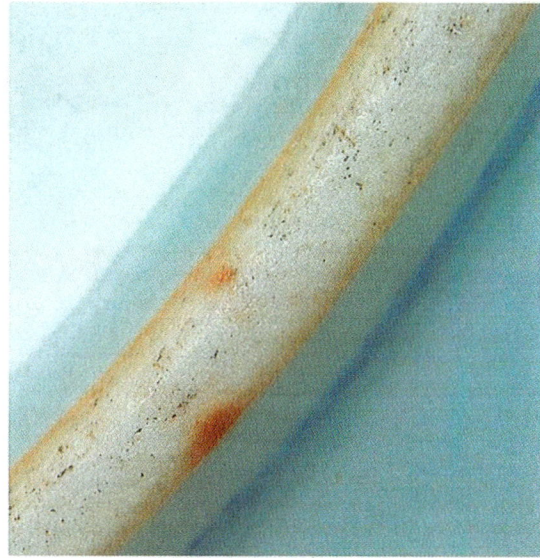

Fig 31.3 Side View of Footrim   *Fig 31.4 Overhead View of Footrim*

The close-up of the character *'Dao'* shows the expected depth of blue, and, as I referred to in my earlier book, the feature which I called 'countable bubbles'. Compare these with the usual modern 'icing sugar' bubble of say *Fig 14.4*, and it will be seen that the modern fakesters have some work to do in the 'bubble area', if their forgeries are not to be detected. Note also the variation in the sizes of these bubbles, which are more noticeable around the edges of the blue.

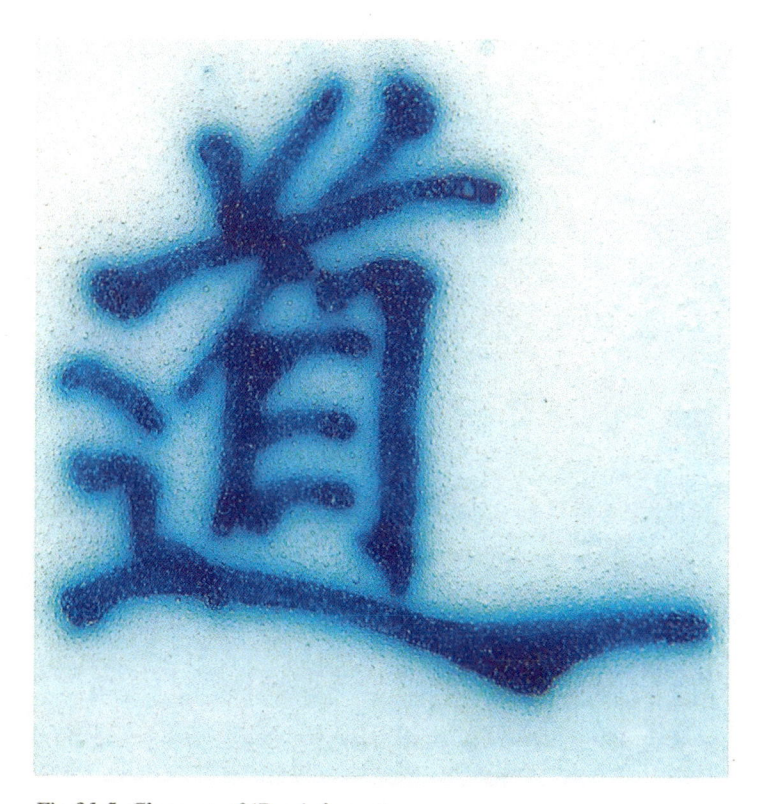

Fig 31.5 Close-up of 'Dao' character

Fig 32.1 Imperial Yellow Bowl, Daoguang Period (1820-1850)

Type: Bowl
Design: Imperial Yellow
Dimensions: 146mm diam
Mark: Daoguang (1820-1850)
Dating: Daoguang

Fig 32.2 Reverse View

The superb yellow bowl *(Fig 32.1)* was undoubtedly made for the Imperial palace, decorated in a colour restricted for the use of the Emperor, the Empress, or the Empress Dowager.

Fig 32.3 Close-up of Imperial Yellow Glaze   *Fig 32.4 Close-up of the Daoguang Mark*

The footrim on this bowl was so perfectly white that I despaired trying to photograph it. The close-up of the yellow glaze *(Fig 32.3)* shows a very fine crackle, and a spattering of darker orange/yellow spots, while in the close-up of the mark *(Fig 32.4)*, we see the very fine calligraphy of the best of the Imperial pieces. The glaze by modern day standards is imperfect, and flaws in the unlevel glaze distinguish this piece from modern copies.

Today's potters are having great difficulty duplicating this colour, I understand, because the old pieces used antimony; which gives off a highly toxic and potentially lethal gas.

Fig 33.1 Snuff Bottles of the Daoguang Period

57

With the restrictions and eventual ban on opium in the Daoguang reign, the practice of snuff-taking arguably reached its height in popularity. Snuff bottles were made both for their practical use and also as a social statement of their owner. The left hand snuff bottle *(Fig 33.1(a))* is a rarity, bearing an underglaze (anhua) decoration of 5-clawed Imperial dragons, while underneath, the seal mark of the ruling Emperor. Little black pinholes of needlepoint fineness dot the unglazed footrim, a recurring feature of some porcelain of this period.

Fig 33.2 Reverse View

However, readers must use these dots as a dating tool with some caution, for I have also seen them appear in porcelains of the early 20th Century. And some Chinese dealers believe, I do not know on what authority, that in the Xuantong reign (1909-1912), old stocks of Daoguang period clay were used to make snuff bottles. Certainly, some snuff bottles are extremely difficult to date unquestionably to either period.

The right hand underglaze bottle appears also to be of the Daoguang period (1820-1850) and I illustrate it to show the curious turned off foot which appears on some of these bottles.

Snuff bottles, of course can be significantly earlier than early 19th Century but 18th Century examples are becoming increasingly difficult (and expensive) to obtain, and for that reason, I have omitted these earlier pieces.

Were it not for the reign marks applied to the undersides of the two saucers of *Fig 34.1*, it would take an expert eye to date them accurately, for the enamels *(Figs 34.3 & 34.4)* are quite similar. The incised (into the glaze) 'family' marks of *Fig 34.2(a)* are a reassuring indicator of age, and I have not seen these marks (yet) applied to modern fakes. They read "Hall of Peace and Harmony". The turquoise enamel of the rock *(Fig 34.1(b))* was an oft-used colour of both the Tongzhi and Guangxu periods, indicating a late 19th Century dating; confirmed by the four character Guangxu mark on the reverse. Probably 40-50 years separate these two saucers.

Fig 34.1 Comparison of Daoguang and Guangxu Enamels

	(a)	(b)
Type:	Saucer	Saucer
Design:	Buddhist Symbols	Safe in a Branch
Dimensions:	110mm diam	133mm diam
Mark:	Daoguang	Guangxu
	(1820-1850)	(1875-1908)
Dating:	Daoguang	Guangxu

Fig 34.2 Reverse View

Fig 34.3 Close-up of Daoguang Period Enamels  *Fig 34.4 Close-up of Guangxu Period Enamels*

Fig 35.1 Comparison of Daoguang and Fake Palace Bowls

Fig 35.1

	(a)	(b)
Type:	Imperial 'Palace' Bowl	Imperial 'Palace' Bowl
Design:	Buddhist Panels on Red Ground	Figural scenes on blue ground
Dimensions:	148mm diam	148mm diam
Mark:	Daoguang (1820-1850)	Daoguang (1820-1850)
Dating:	Daoguang	20th Century (see text)

60

The colour of the underglaze blue of the 'Palace' bowl *(Fig 35.1(a))* appears to be unique to the period, and potters have attempted without success to duplicate this colour, both in the early part of the 20th Century, and again in modern times; as the neighbouring bowl *(Fig 35.1(b))* shows.

The blue ground bowl (one of a pair) was sold by Sothebys as circa 1900, but while the underglaze blue mark appears to be of the late Qing or early Republic period, the enamels, in my opinion, are late 20th Century.

It is interesting to compare the beautiful calligraphy of the genuine bowl *(Fig 35.3)* with the comparatively crude attempt on the reproduction.

This mark is the earliest I have seen to date which exhibits the 'hollow line' feature, probably indicating that it was made in the final years of the reign; circa 1850. Note also the uneven dimpled glaze.

Had it not been for the fact that this bowl has been broken in two, it would be beyond my usual budget, its undamaged retail value at the time of writing being in the vicinity of $US8,000 to $10,000.

Fig 35.2 Reverse View

Fig 35.3 Imperial Reign Mark of the Daoguang Period *Fig 35.4 Daoguang Reign Mark on a 20th Century copy*

In *Fig 35.4*, the close-up photography shows the 'icing sugar' bubbles and even glaze, so common to many of these modern reproductions. The enamel close-ups *(Figs 35.5 & 35.6)* are shown for comparison.

The underglaze blue colour is also 'wrong', but it will take a trained eye to identify this bowl as fake, from that one feature alone.

Fig 35.5 Daoguang Imperial Enamels

Fig 35.6 Modern Enamels Copying Daoguang

Fig 36.1

Type:	Plate
Design:	Iron Red & Green Enamel Scrolls
Dimensions:	233mm diam
Mark:	Daoguang (1820-1850)
Dating:	Daoguang

One of the big problems for collectors today is the Chinese practice of applying later overglaze iron red enamel reign marks on porcelains made in the period of the mark. It is therefore reassuring to find a rare underglaze blue reign mark, as this must have been fired prior to the enamel decoration. The plate (or shallow dish) of *Fig 36.1*, has a curious combination of iron red and green enamels, of relatively low quality, typical of the domestic porcelains of the Daoguang period.

Again we see the distinctive greyish blue glaze, iron orange edge to the footrim, and obvious imperfections in the glaze coverage of the underside.

Fig 36.2 Reverse View

The close-up of the enamels *(Fig 36.3)* do not in my opinion show features that are very helpful in dating. However, if one compares these enamels with say those of the Kangxi period *(Fig 12.4)*, it will be seen that the black enamel outline and vein, are now painted on top of the green, instead of underneath it; undoubtedly because the later enamels are opaque and not translucent.

The close-up of the mark *(Fig 36.4)* shows a deep glaze over the blue, a myriad of small bubbles, and a glaze eruption adjacent to the lower edge.

Fig 36.3 Close-up of Daoguang Period Enamels   *Fig 36.4 Close-up of Daoguang 'Minyao' Reign Mark*

Fig 37.1 Carved Porcelains (See text) - Collection of Geoffrey C Perkins

The Daoguang period is known for its carved porcelains, and arguably the most renowned potter in this field is Wang Bingrong. It remains a matter of some debate as to whether Wang Bingrong actually worked in the Daoguang reign, as many of his works (and *Fig 37.1(a) & (b)* are examples) would seem to date to the Tongzhi period, or even the later Guangxu era. In any event, judging by the number of pieces made, Wang Bingrong was probably a factory name, rather than an individual potter. Gerald Davison, for example, author of *"The Handbook of Marks on Chinese Ceramics"*, states Wang Bingrong to be a Daoguang period mark. If this is the case, then Wang must have been very old when the yellow ginger jar was made, for it is almost identical in shape and body (see the inside of the lids) as the neighbouring green ginger jar; and the latter has an underglaze incised 'China' mark, indicating a date of manufacture after 1891.

The placement of these pieces in the Daoguang section of this book is a mistake on my part, as with the exception of the 116mm high right hand brush pot *(Fig 37.1(d))* which is a modern copy, all three in my view date to the second half of the 19th Century.

Fig 37.2 Reverse View

I mention also the carved porcelain fakes being made today, an example of which I illustrate later in this book *(Fig 132.5)*. This particular piece did not from memory have a Wang Bingrong mark, but the factory had a genuine marked brush pot which they had previously used as a model, and was probably responsible for the fake brushpot which I knowingly purchased in 1997 *(Fig 37.1(d))*.

I have seen these modern fakes sell in reputable English auctions for as much as £1300.

Fig 38.1 Enamelled Celadons of the Early 19th Century

	(a)	(b)	(c)
Type:	Plate	Saucer	Plate
Design:	Peaches 'Over the Rim'	Erotic Scene	Peaches 'Over the Rim'
Dimensions:	180mm diam	133mm diam	180mm diam
Mark:	Pseudo Reign Mark (& Incised Owner's Mark)	Pseudo Reign Mark	Pseudo Reign Mark
Dating:	Daoguang	Daoguang	Daoguang

In selecting the three enamelled celadons *(Fig 38.1)* to illustrate, I am treading on fairly dangerous ground, for I could gain little consensus among the expert Chinese dealers shown these pieces. In my view, the porcelain dates to the Daoguang period (1820-1850), but I cannot say the same about the enamelling. I believe the enamelling to be modern, as is evidenced by the crack in the close-up *(Fig 38.2)*, which disappears under the enamel. These old celadons have been much used, and as in these examples, the chipped and fritted edges have been turned off, and the cavettos polished. The signs of genuine wear, not visible in this photograph, extend only as far as the enamels, reinforcing my view that they are later applied.

Fig 38.2 Modern? Enamels on old porcelain (see text)

The reverse of these pieces also show an underglaze blue pseudo reign mark, another practice which was not uncommon in the first half of the 19th Century.

Please bear in mind that this dating is my own opinion, yet to be confirmed by some authoritative reference source.

CHAPTER FOUR
XIANFENG REIGN
(1850-1861)

The Xianfeng reign (1850-1861) is generally regarded as the low point in Chinese ceramic history, and it is extremely difficult to obtain Xianfeng mark and period examples.

Fig 39.1 Rare Xianfeng Period Mortar, Dated 1851

Type: Mortar
Design: Underglaze Blue Calligraphy
Dimensions: 115mm diam
Mark: Dated inscription to 1851
Dating: Circa 1851

Even rarer to find are underglaze blue pieces bearing an exact reference to a particular year; in the case of the mortar *(Fig 39.1)*, 1851.

The underside *(Fig 39.2)* shows a continuation of the iron orange edge to the footrim, so common to the Daoguang period, while the thick bluish glaze could be mistaken for the 18th Century. The Xianfeng mark *(Fig 39.3)* is covered with a thick bubbled glaze, possibly necessary to cover and conceal the poorly levigated open body, shown in *Fig 39.4*. Note that this latter photograph is of the well-worn inside of the mortar, no doubt repeatedly battered with a pestle, for it has entirely lost the iron orange colour of the underside *(Fig 39.5)*.

Fig 39.2 Reverse View

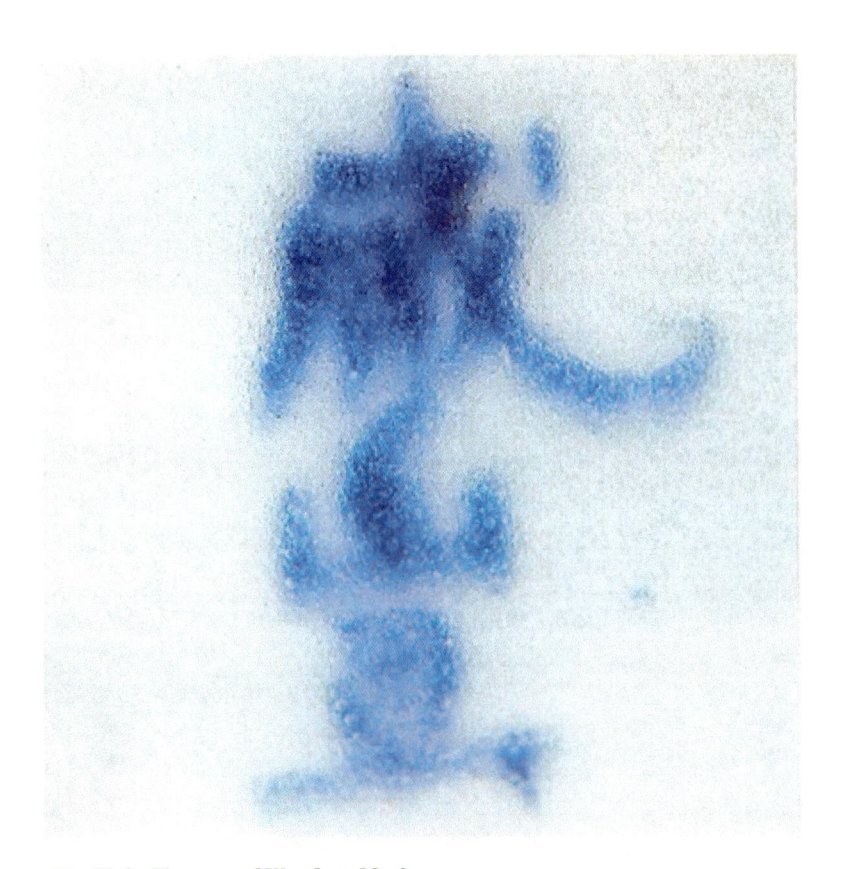

Fig 39.3 Close-up of Xianfeng Mark

Fig 39.4 Close-up of Inside *Fig 39.5 Close-up of Underside*

Fig 40.1 Xianfeng Marked Enamelled Porcelain

	(a)	(b)
Type:	Plate	Saucer (Japanese?)
Design:	Floral	Satsuma
Dimensions:	240mm diam	153mm diam
Mark:	Xianfeng (1851-1861)	Xianfeng (1851-1861)
Dating:	Xianfeng	Second half 19th Century

Fig 40.2 Reverse View

The left hand plate *(Fig 40.1(a))* bears a Xianfeng mark (1851-1861), which in my view is contemporary with the plate's date of manufacture. It can be very difficult detecting a later applied mark, as often the only assurance of an old mark may be the imperfections in the iron red enamel.

The neighbouring saucer is a real curiosity, as it appears to me to be of Japanese origin and design, perhaps made by an enterprising Japanese potter, capitalising on the closure of the Jingdezhen kilns in 1855.

The body of the Chinese plate shown *Fig 40.4* is roughly levigated, while the enamels *(Fig 40.5)* are distinctly muddy and unappealing.

Fig 40.3 Xianfeng Enamel Mark

Fig 40.4 Close-up of Xianfeng Footrim

Fig 40.5 Close-up of Xianfeng Enamels

Fig 41.1 Porcelains of the Mid-19th Century

The tea caddies and apple-shaped brush washer *(Fig 41.1)* could date to either the Daoguang or Xianfeng periods. Each is characterised with a similar coarsely levigated body and an iron orange edge to a thick bubbly glaze. Historically most Chinese dealers date these as Daoguang period, but in my view, a mid-19th Century dating is more appropriate.

Fig 100.1 Modern Day Artist Signed and Dated Porcelains

There have been numerous new innovations throughout the Post-Mao period, arguably the most important being the development of the 'eggshell' thin porcelains. The vase *(Fig 98.1)* is another example, being plain white in appearance until it is lit from the inside; revealing blue and red secret decoration. I have also seen green.

The traditional shapes and colours remain popular, and the modern day snuff bottles *(Fig 99.1)* will usually be found with an apocryphal Qianlong mark, even though there was probably never an original Qianlong mark and period snuff bottle made with any of these designs or shapes.

Today, it is gratifying to see that the artists are being encouraged to experiment with new shapes, designs and techniques of decoration, despite the pitifully low incomes that all but the most senior ones receive. I took a fancy to the two freely drawn plates *(Fig 100.1)*, on my visit to Jingdezhen in April 1998, and acquired them for 50RMB (about $US6) each.

I also purchased, but from different factories, the superbly decorated vase and teapot of *Fig 101.1 & 102.1*. There can be no question that the modern factories have the ability to duplicate the quality of the best of the 18th Century Imperial porcelains; but not exactly enough to fool the expert, who will note the slightly garish and shiny enamels, the wrong shade of turquoise, and the traditional artificial 'ageing' of the footrim.

CHAPTER FIVE
TONGZHI REIGN
(1861-1875)

As I stated earlier, according to Bushell, the Taiping rebels were not expelled from Jingdezhen until 1864, and the Imperial Factory was rebuilt two years later.

The Imperial saucer of *Fig 42.1* must therefore date between 1866 and 1875. Apart from two minor kiln flaws, this saucer is almost perfect, as is (unusually), the reverse.

Particularly to note is the superb quality of the calligraphy, the smooth ridged foot, and the faint yellow line abutting the glaze.

Curiously the mark on this saucer is 180 degrees exactly out of rotation; yet further evidence of the unreliability of any 'rule' in Chinese porcelain.

Fig 42.1 Imperial Saucer, Tongzhi Period

The base of this saucer must have been covered in a very thin glaze, for the blue has burst to the surface in a number of places.

Fig 42.2 Reverse View

Fig 42.3 Tongzhi Imperial Mark

Fig 42.4 Tongzhi Imperial Footrim

Fig 43.1 Dated Porcelains of the Tongzhi Period

	(a)	(b)
Type:	Chopstick Drainer	Censer
Design:	Landscape	Four-clawed Dragons
Dimensions:	145mmH x 123mmW	200mmH x 243mmW
Mark:	Dated 1871	Dated last month 1874
	Made by Wei Zi Yu	
Dating:	Circa 1871	Circa 1874

In *Fig 43.1*, one can see the difference in coloured glazes and underglaze blue available in the Tongzhi reign. The chopstick drainer bears a dated inscription to 1871, with holes at rear and in the base, may, prior to firing, have been a brushpot. These are very uncommon to say the least, and with a dated inscription, quite rare.

Censers of the type shown *(Fig 43.1(b))* were regular gifts to a person's local temple, and they provide an important clue to dating, as they often bear a dated inscription.

The bodies on these more utilitarian wares were poorly levigated, and as the close-ups of *Fig 43.3 & 43.4* show, turning off the base caused larger pieces of the body material to be dislodged.

The chopstick holder, by comparison with the censer, has been quite thinly glazed, the latter's mark covered by a mass of very fine bubbles *(Fig 43.5 & 43.6)*.

Fig 43.2 Reverse View

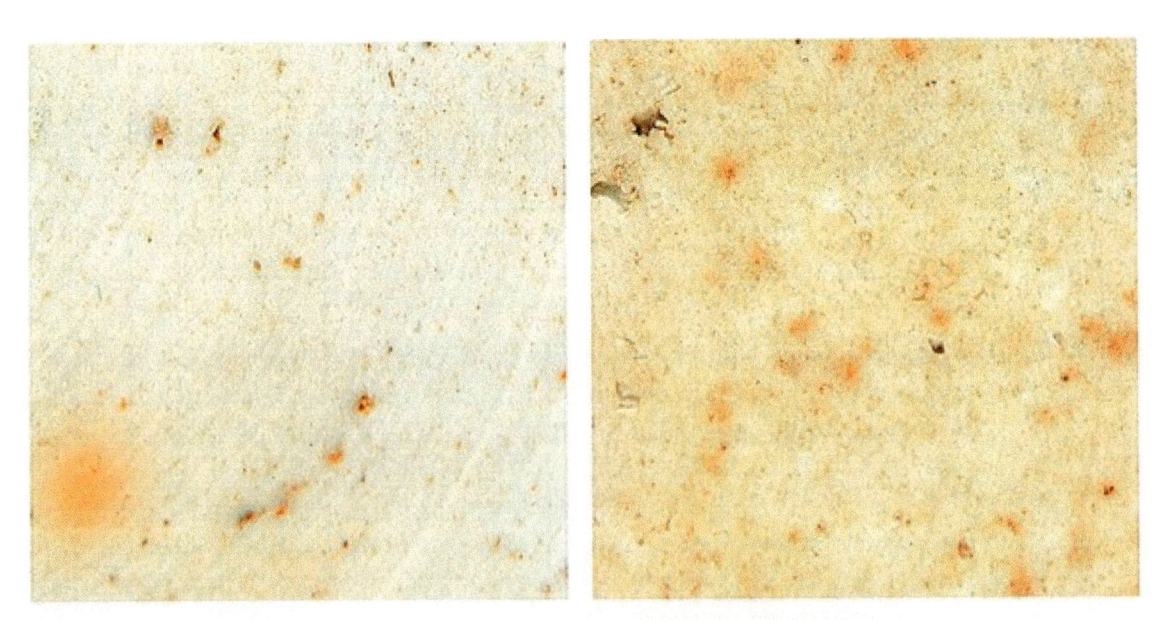

Fig 43.3 Base of Fig 43.1(a)

Fig 43.4 Base of Fig 43.1(b)

Fig 43.5 Close-up of Mark on Fig 43.1(a)

Fig 43.6 Close-up of Mark on Fig 43.1(b)

The two yellow ground saucers *(Fig 44.1)*, are, like those shown in *Fig 11.1*, made for a fifth rank concubine. The Tongzhi Emperor died at a relatively young age, and this type of ware is consequently quite rare in this reign.

Fig 44.1 Tongzhi Imperial Enamelled Porcelains

Type: Saucers
Design: Green & Aubergine Dragons on a Yellow Ground
Dimensions: 131mm diam
Mark: Tongzhi (1861-1875)
Dating: Tongzhi

The close-up of the footrim *(Fig 44.2)*, shows again the "ridge in the roundedness" and a finely levigated body.

There appear to have been at least three distinct ways of applying the reign mark on yellow porcelains in the late Qing, a feature I have not previously seen mentioned.

One was to apply an overglaze aubergine enamel, which almost invariably fired brown. Another was to apply an underglaze mark (probably cobalt blue), which when mixed with the yellow glaze, also fired brown.

Fig 44.2 Close-up of Footrim

The third was an underglaze blue mark under a white glaze. I have also seen incised marks under a yellow glaze, but while some of these may prove to be genuinely of the period, most in my opinion should be viewed with suspicion.

Fig 45.1 Enamelled 'minyao' Porcelains of the Tongzhi Period

	(a)	(b)	(c)	(d)
Type:	Stem Dish	Stem Dish	Tea Bowl	Tea Bowl
Design:	Iron Red Bats	Figural	Floral	Floral
Dimensions:	95mm diam	82mm diam	92mm diam	83mm diam
Mark:	Tongzhi (1861-1875)	Tongzhi (1861-1875) Dated inscription 1886	Tongzhi (1861-1875)	Tongzhi (1861-1875)
Dating:	Tongzhi	Tongzhi	Tongzhi	Tongzhi

Fig 45.2 Reverse View

The two little stem dishes and two tea bowls of *Fig 45.1* are representative of the minyao ("people's ware") made in the Tongzhi reign. Masses of these crudely decorated and potted stem dishes were made bearing a Tongzhi mark, and it seems possible to me that they were made in a city other than Jingdezhen, to satisfy the porcelain demand while that city was under Taiping control. This I stress is speculation, and has not been confirmed.

The close-ups of *Fig 45.3 & 45.4* show two distinctly different bodies, one crudely trimmed and yellowish, the other better trimmed and grey.

The little dish *(Fig 45.1(b))* bears in addition to a Tongzhi (1861-1875) reign mark, a dated inscription to autumn 1886; at least 11 years after the date indicated by the reign mark. I will illustrate several such pieces with conflicting dates, but in this instance, it would seem that the dated inscription was later applied; ie, the potting was done earlier.

I am certain not everyone will agree with my conclusion.

Fig 45.3 Close-up of Footrim of Fig 45.1(a)

Fig 45.4 Close-up of Footrim of Fig 45.1(d)

Fig 46.1 Lidded Bowls of the Tongzhi Period

	(a)	(b)	(c)
Type:	Bowl on Stand	Lidded Bowl	Lidded Bowl
Design:	Figural Panels on a Blue Ground	Stamped Longevity Characters	Blue Enamel Branches
Dimensions:	102mm diam	105mm diam	100mm diam
Mark:	Tongzhi (1861-1875)	Tongzhi (1861-1875)	Tongzhi (1861-1875)
Dating:	Tongzhi	Tongzhi	Tongzhi

The three lidded bowls *(Fig 46.1)* all bear an iron red Tongzhi seal mark, and my examination of the impurities in the iron red enamel suggest to me that they are mark and period. Having said that, one experienced Hong Kong dealer (who sold me the bowl) says the central stamped bowl was made in the 1930s. The base mark evidently bears the name Wong, but interested readers may do their own translation from the photograph.

Fig 46.2 Reverse View

The close-up of the enamels *(Fig 46.3)* of the left hand bowl, show in addition to signs of genuine wear, the concentration of burst 'pinhole' bubbles which is a feature of the 19th Century blue enamel.

Fig 46.3 Close-up of Enamels (Fig 46.1(a))

Fig 47.1 Enamelled Porcelains of the Tongzhi Period

	(a)	(b)	(c)	(d)
Type:	Soap Dish	Saucer	Brush Pot	Saucer
Design:	Rooster	Floral Panels	HoHo Bird	Flowers
Dimensions:	122mmL	135mm diam	118m H	136mm diam
Mark:	Tongzhi (1861-1875)	Tongzhi (1861-1875)	Tongzhi (1861-1875)	Tongzhi (1861-1875)
Dating:	Tongzhi	Tongzhi	Tongzhi	Tongzhi

Fig 47.2 Reverse View

In *Fig 47.1*, I have shown four Tongzhi marked porcelains, all of which, in my opinion, are of the period. There is debate in some quarters that the soap dish is a cricket cage. This one had remains of soap in the holes. Note the greyish/white glazes and poorly levigated footrims. The right hand saucer is extremely unusual, being potted with ten sides; a decagon.

Fig 47.3 Enamels of Fig 47.1(b)

Fig 47.4 Enamels of Fig 47.1(c)

The three close-ups of the enamel decoration show the expected impurities, the absence of which in many instances will identify immediately the modern reproduction.

Fig 47.5 Enamels of Fig 47.1(a)

The three tubular vases *(Fig 48.1)* are especially interesting. There are various arguments as to what their purpose was. Initially, this shape may have held arrows (hence the name arrow vase), but they may also have been used to hold painting brushes or scrolls. In the early 19th Century, the 'breathing' holes were cut into them, and their use adapted to hat stands; as *Fig 48.3* illustrates.

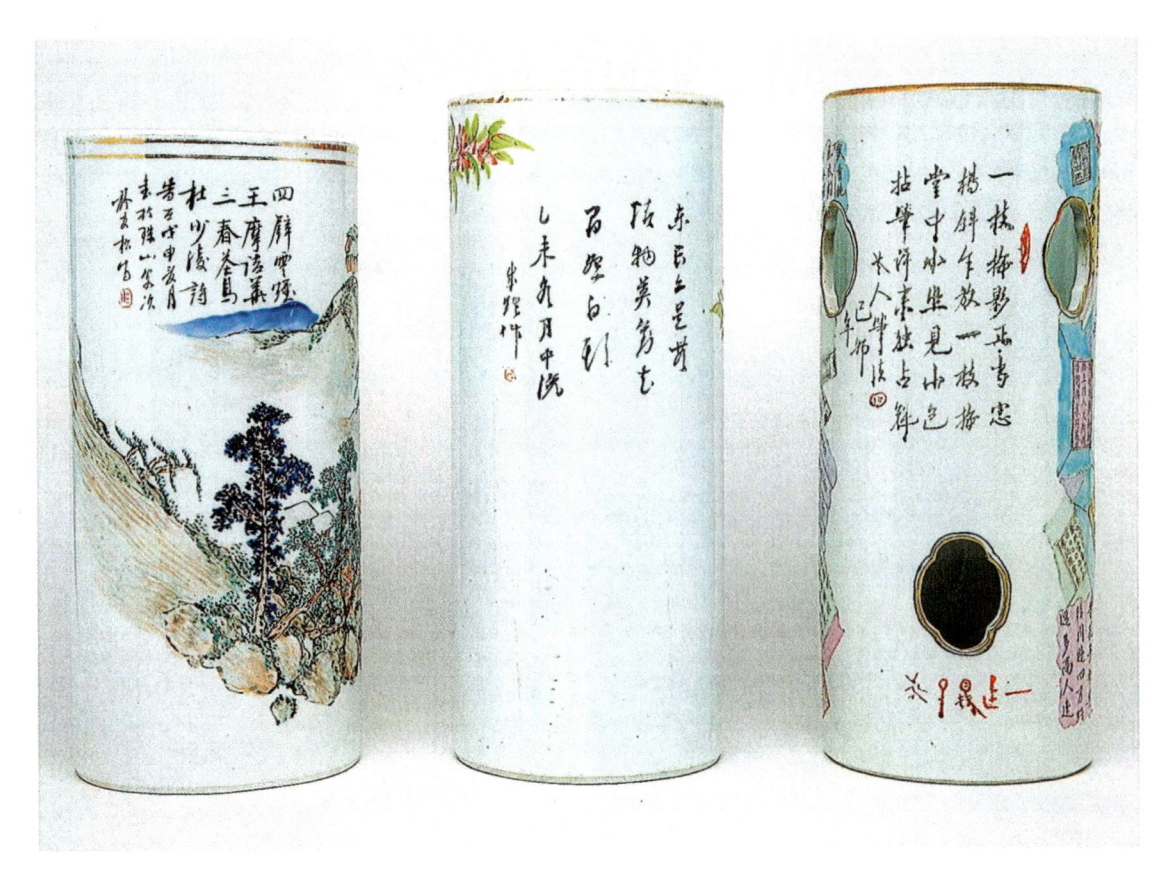

Fig 48.1 Tubular Vases (Hat Stands) of the Late Qing Dynasty

	(a)	(b)	(c)
Type:	Tubular Vase	Tubular Vase	Hat Stand
Design:	Mountain Scene	Bird in a Branch	Banners
Dimensions:	267mm H	282mm H	282mm H
Mark:	Tongzhi (1861-1875)	Guangxu (1875-1908)	Qianlong (1736-1795)
Inscription Date:	1908	1895	1915
Dating:	Tongzhi	Guangxu	Early Republic
Collection:			Geoffrey C Perkins

My very good friend, Mr Tai of Hop Wah Antiques in Hong Kong, is absolutely adamant that the Qianjiang enamels of *Fig 48.1(a)* are Guangxu period, not Tongzhi (see p137). I am equally adamant that the porcelain body is Tongzhi period, as is the base mark, suggesting that this piece may have remained as an undecorated blank for at least 33 years; as the inscription is dated 1908.

The central piece *(Fig 48.1(b))* bears a Guangxu (1875-1908) base mark, and an inscription dated 1895, while the right hand hat stand *(Fig 48.1(c))* has a Qianlong (1736-1795) base mark and an inscription dated 1915. I have owned a smaller brushpot with this decoration, but bearing a Tongzhi mark.

If I may be permitted a slight digression from the subject, the hat and queue is an interesting historical relic. During the Boxer uprising of 1900, many Chinese cut off their hated queues, which were in their eyes a symbol of the Manchu domination. When the uprising was suppressed, some Chinese resorted to stitching a false queue under their hat, in an endeavour to conceal their Boxer allegiance. These queues were, as in this case, made from young girls' hair.

Fig 48.2 Reverse View

Fig 48.3 Base View

Fig 48.4 Enamel Close-up of Fig 48.1(a)

Fig 48.5 Enamel Close-up of Fig 48.1(b)

The close-ups of the enamels *(Fig 48.4, 48.5 & 48.6)* may assist readers in dating unmarked porcelains of the same period.

In *Fig 49.1*, I have illustrated four pieces from the late Qing Dynasty, the first three of which all bear a Tongzhi reign mark. The upturned beaker *(Fig 49.1(d))* may be a little later.

Fig 48.6 Enamel Close-up of Fig 48.1(c)

Fig 49.1 Enamelled Porcelains of the Late Qing

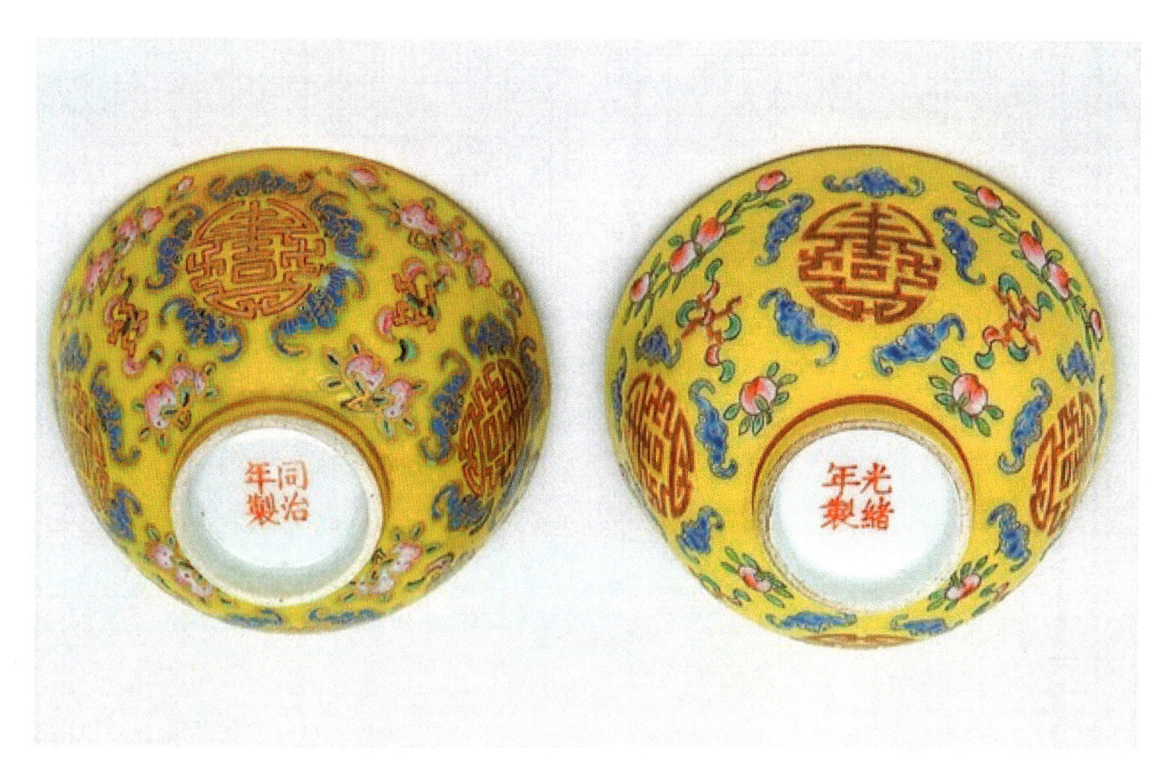

Fig 50.1 Tongzhi Imperial Wedding Bowl & New Reproduction (inverted)

	(a)	(b)
Type:	Tea Bowl	Tea Bowl
Design:	Bats & Long Life Symbols	Bats & Long Life Symbols
Dimensions:	67mm diam	66mm diam
Mark:	Tongzhi (1861-1875)	Guangxu (1875-1908)
Dating:	Tongzhi	Modern, Circa 1997

The delightful little yellow bowl of *Fig 50.1(a)* is of a pattern which was made for the Tongzhi Emperor's wedding in 1872. This was the first Imperial wedding since the Kangxi Emperor's, over 200 years earlier (the previous Emperors had married prior to accession), and the Chinese historical records state that 7294 pieces were made in ten sets. Ronald W Longsdorf, in an article in the October 1996 issue of Orientations, identifies 13 sets, not 10.

In the two close-up photographs of the marks *(Fig 50.2 & 50.3)*, one can see the impurities in the genuine Tongzhi iron red enamel, while the neighbouring fake shows none.

In *Fig 50.4 & 50.5*, we can see the disparity between the genuine Tongzhi period enamels and the modern fakes. Note the absence of gilding to the bats on the fake, and white eyes instead of black and green. The modern day yellow enamel is a beautiful lustrous colour, which I am certain will become tomorrow's antique, but it is different in comparison with the original; just too good.

Fig 50.2 Close-up of Tongzhi Mark

Fig 50.3 Close-up of Fake Guangxu Mark

Fig 50.4 Enamel Close-up - Tongzhi

Fig 50.5 Enamel Close-up - Modern

CHAPTER SIX
GUANGXU REIGN
(1875-1908)

The Chinese historical records are abysmally silent on the porcelain of the Guangxu reign. Liu records (p 35) that from Guangxu onwards, Ming-sha kaolin from Mt Kaoling was used in the Imperial factory. Fortunately, we have the extremely helpful analyses and commentary of Scherzer & Vogt, for in 1882, they recorded four kinds of kaolin, coming, and I quote, "from Ki-men, Si-ho, Hing-tze, and Tong-hang", and they analysed both the Ki-men and Tong-hang samples.

The Tong-hang sample (which was the same as that studied by Ebelman & Salvetat almost 40 years earlier) had an iron-oxide (Fe_2O_3) content over three times higher than the Ming-cha (Ki-men) kaolin, giving it a yellowish shade when fired. The Ming-cha or Ming-sha kaolin had of course been used in the Imperial factory from circa 1600 to 1800, and this is undoubtedly the primary reason why so many fakes of the late Qing and early Republic periods remain accepted as genuine 17th or 18th Century pieces.

To assist in their detection and recategorisation, I have illustrated a number of genuine Guangxu period footrims, together with copies from the modern day.

Fig 51.1. Guanyao & Guanguyao Porcelains of the Guangxu Reign

	(a)	(b)
Type:	Saucer	Plate
Design:	Imperial Dragons	Imperial Dragons (Reverse decorated)
Dimensions:	165mm diam	252mm diam
Mark:	Guangxu (1875-1908)	Guangxu (1875-1908)
Dating:	Guangxu	Guangxu

Fig 51.2   Reverse View

The Imperial saucer dish *(Fig 51.1(a))* is a superb example of the best underglaze blue of this period. Comparison with the neighbouring plate *(Fig 51.1(b))* shows subtle differences in quality, probably indicating that the plate was made to order for one of the wealthy Chinese aristocracy. Both the marks and the footrims and the finishing of the underside, show this lesser quality. The academics refer to these 'custom-ordered' porcelains as 'Guanguyao', many of which must have originated from the Imperial factory.

Fig 51.3 Imperial Footrim - Guangxu   *Fig 51.4 Non-Imperial Footrim - Guangxu*

Readers who have my earlier book may like to compare this plate with the previously illustrated fake (Fig 55(a)).

Fig 51.5 Close-up of Guangxu Imperial Mark (Xu Character)

Fig 51.6 Close-up of Guangxu Non-Imperial Mark (Xu Character)

Fig 52.1 Comparison of Genuine Guangxu and Fake Vases

	(a)	(b)
Type:	Vase	Vase
Design:	Hawthorn (Cracked Ice)	Dragon
Dimensions:	180mm H	185mm H
Mark:	Guangxu (1875-1908)	Guangxu (1875-1908)
Dating:	Guangxu	Fourth Quarter 20th Century

The close-ups of the marks *(Fig 51.5 & 51.6)* show clearly the 'countable bubbles' which I referred to in my earlier book. Note also the traces of 'hollow line', the variations in colour, and the variations in bubble size.

These are reassuring features for ascribing a genuine Guangxu mark and period dating.

Vases bearing underglaze blue reign marks of the period are a relative rarity, a minyao piece possibly rarer than the guanyao (Imperial). The hawthorn or cracked ice patterned vase *(Fig 52.1(a))* is such a piece.

I am uncertain of the exact age of its neighbouring vase *(Fig 52.1(b))*, as I purchased this in an English auction in 1996. There can be little doubt however that it is a relatively modern copy.

Fig 52.2 Reverse View

Fig 52.3 Footrim of Fig 52.1(a)

Fig 52.4 Footrim of Fig 52.1(b) (Fake)

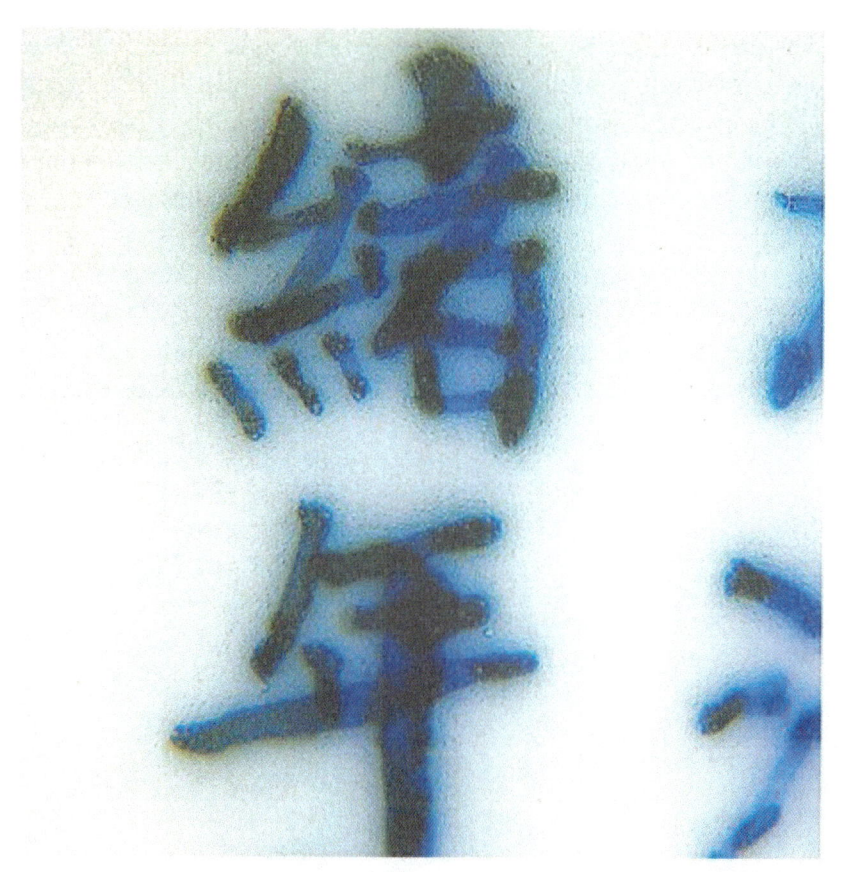

Fig 52.5 Close-up of Mark of Fig 52.1(a)

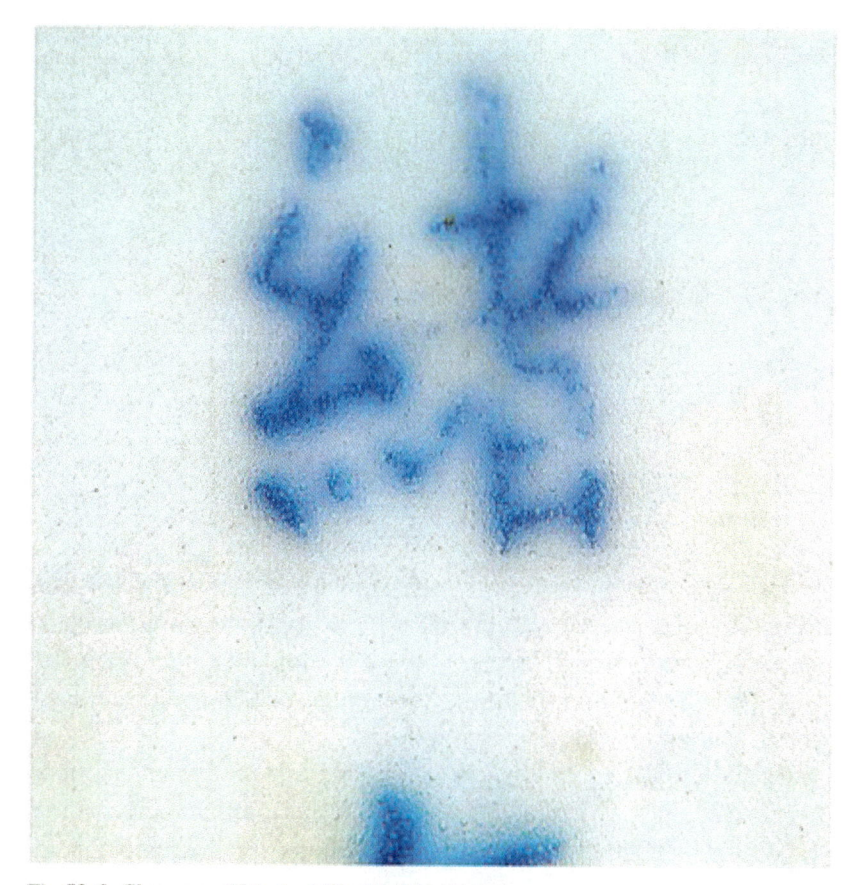

Fig 52.6 Close-up of Mark of Fig 52.1(b) (Fake)

The fake vase of Fig 52.1(b) would fool all but the most experienced dealers.

The trained eye would immediately be on the alert from the shape and the colour of the blue. Closer inspection would reveal an artificially tinted bluish glaze and (after cleaning), a too white body. The close-up view of the mark of the genuine vase *(Fig 52.5)* reveals the usual Guangxu bubbling (countable but for the fact that the cobalt is almost black).

While the copyist has almost successfully produced a 'countable bubble' glaze, the underglaze blue mark in close-up *(Fig 52.6)*, appears almost to have been lost.

Another point to note on this vase is the excessive shine, a feature which, as I have previously mentioned, the copyist may attempt to dull with acid or scratching.

Fig 53.1 Comparison of Genuine Guangxu Bowl with Modern Copy

	(a)	(b)
Type:	Rice Bowl	Rice Bowl
Design:	Lotus	Lotus
Dimensions:	105mm diam	107mm diam
Mark:	Guangxu (1875-1908)	Guangxu (1875-1908)
Dating:	Guangxu	Circa 1997

It was really only in relatively recent times that the modern day fakesters attempted to copy genuine Guangxu period porcelains. Many (but I stress not all) of the Guangxu marked fakes from say 1965 to 1990 did not follow a known Guangxu design; for example, from the List of 1900. This meant that the experienced dealer could readily identify them by their shape, or design, or mix of enamels.

The right hand fake lotus design bowl *(Fig 53.1(b))* has fooled a number of experienced dealers, but when it is placed alongside a genuine Guangxu period example, the potter's 'errors' are readily discernible: a too blue glaze which has been chemically dulled and an artificially grey footrim which shows a 'too white' body below.

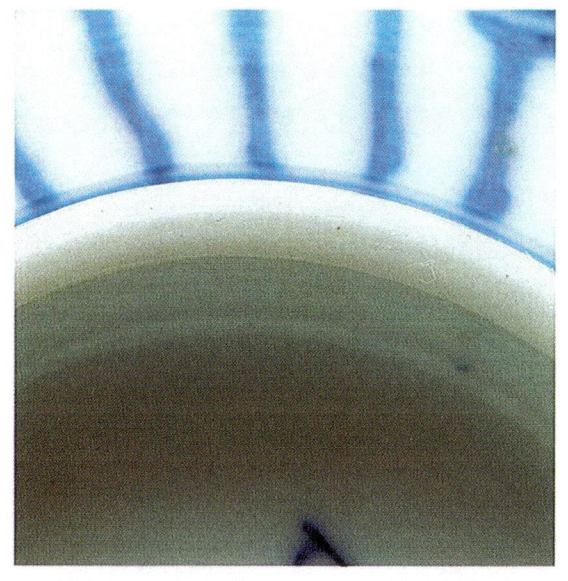

Fig 53.2 Close-up of Guangxu Foot of Fig 53.1(a)    *Fig 53.3 Close-up of Fake Foot of Fig 53.1(b)*

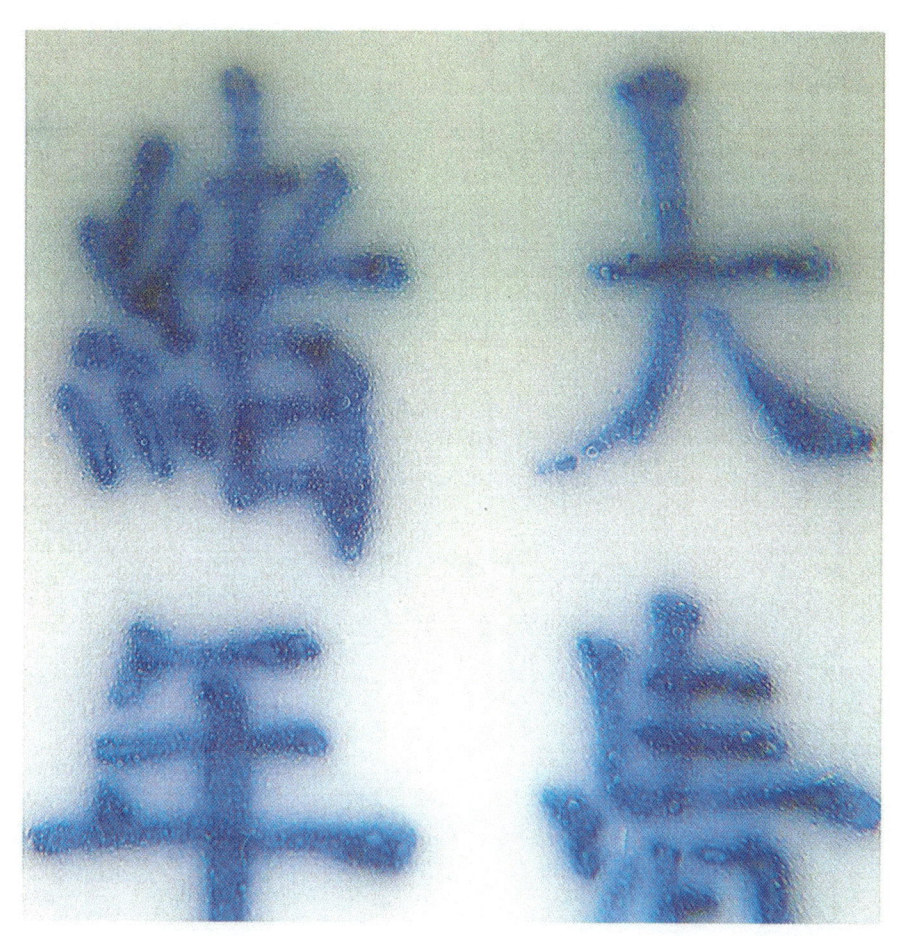

Fig 53.4 Close-up of Guangxu Mark of Fig 53.1(a)

Note the 'split line' feature of many genuine Guangxu underglaze blue marks *(Fig 53.4)*, together with the variations in density of the blue.

The bubbles of the glaze in the fake *(Fig 53.5)* are again like 'icing sugar' by comparison, and the marks are of a generally uniform depth of colour.

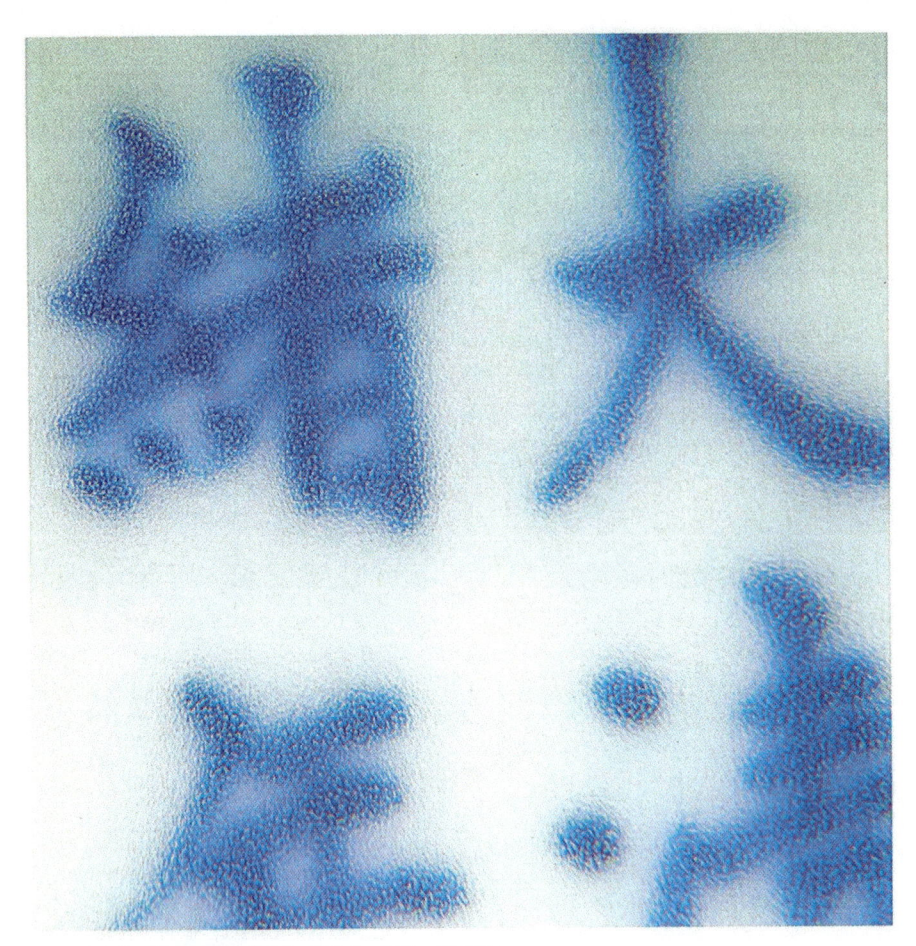

Fig 53.5 Close-up of Fake Mark of Fig 53.1(b)

Fig 54.1 Underglaze Blue Porcelains of the Guangxu Period

The range of blue colours available to the Guangxu potters can be seen in the examples illustrated *(Fig 54.1)*.

The two left hand wine cups are dated 1907, and the adjoining two are in my view of similar date. The central lower sauce dish bears the remains of a Chinese Government 'Approved for Export' seal. Readers should note that these seals are also applied to pieces of a modern date, ie: they are no guarantee of age.

Some Guangxu blue and white porcelain had a tendency to frit, a problem which besieged the 18th Century potters, possibly a defect attributable to the Mt Kaoling kaolin. The lower right sauce dish shows this fritting around the edges, and also, unusually for these pieces, a thick 'orange peel' glaze.

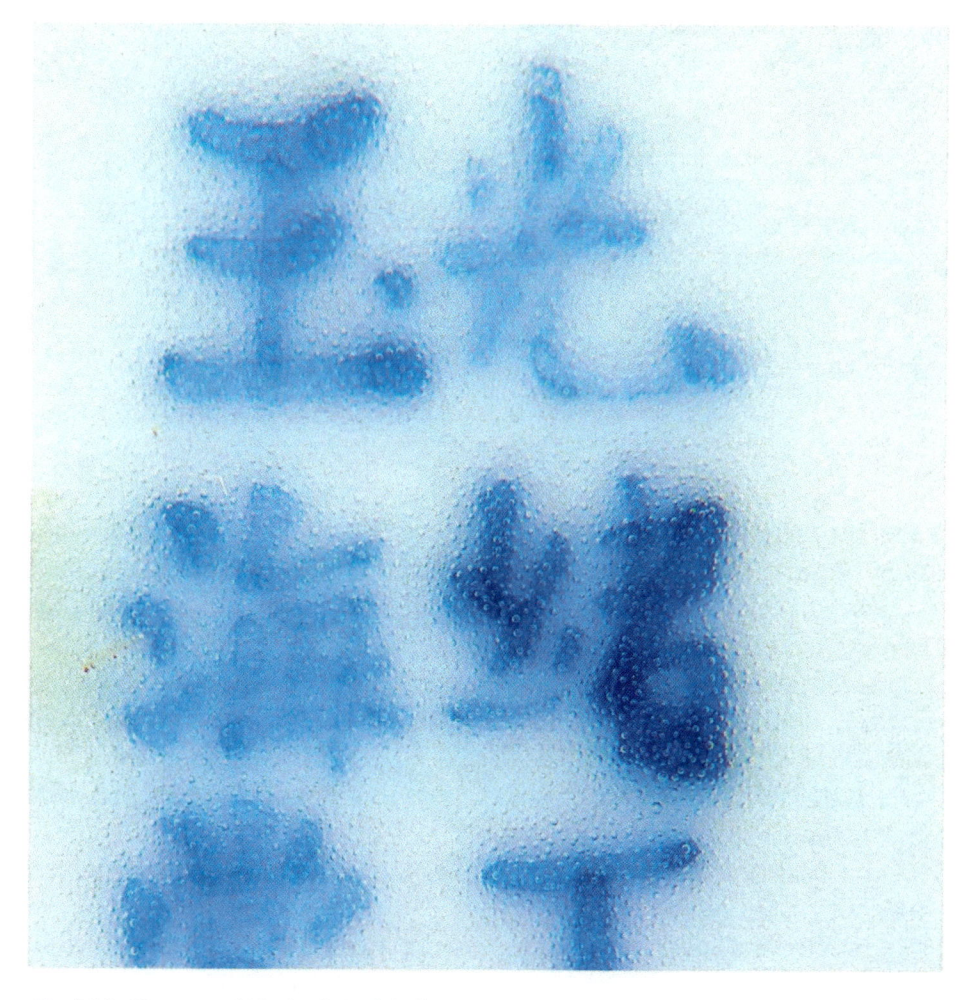

Fig 54.2 Close-up of Mark of Fig 54.1(b)

The mark *(Fig 54.2)* is 'classic' Guangxu period; unmistakable for the 'countable bubbles', variations in density of the blue, and 'hollow lines'.

Readers should by now be starting to recognise these late Qing features, and the four examples *(Fig 55.1)* are further variants of the period.

Fig 55.1 Underglaze Blue Porcelains of the Guangxu Period

I deliberately omitted the dimensions of these multiple illustrations. For those interested, the wine cup *(Fig 54.1(a))* is 80mm diam, and the bowl *(Fig 55.1(a))* 175mm diam.

The ricegrain decoration, popular in the 18th Century, returned again in quantity and much of it bore the marks of the ruling Guangxu Emperor.

Four character underglaze blue Guangxu marks are a relative rarity, and the reason for affixing a Guangxu reign mark to the little tubular censer escapes me. Perhaps it was in admiration of the Emperor.

Also rare is the mark on the base of the top left hand bowl *(Fig 55.1(a))* which reads 'Imitation Antique'.

This dragon decorated bowl does not bear either a reign or date mark, but it must date from this period, in my view, circa 1890.

Here the number of claws gives a clue, for most of the early Republic dragons are decorated with the five claws of the former Imperial dragon; the Emperor having by that time been dethroned.

I took the opportunity to illustrate the roughly levigated footrim of the censer *(Fig 55.2)* in order that it may be compared with the fake, earlier illustrated *(Fig 52.4)*; but on reflection, it really isn't much assistance.

The close-up of the dragon scale decoration on the bowl *(Fig 55.3)* shows again several features of the late Qing underglaze blue porcelains; the 'cross-hatch and dot' method of depicting dragon scales, the bubble burst (actually cobalt erupting through the glaze) and of course, 'hollow line'.

98

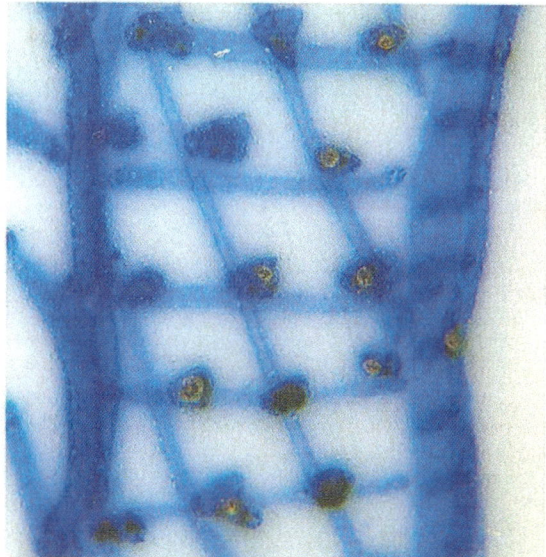

Fig 55.2 Footrim of Censer (Fig 55.1(c))   *Fig 55.3 Close-up of Dragon Scales from Fig 55.1(a)*

On my visit to Jingdezhen in April 1998, I managed to obtain a few sherds from the Imperial kiln site, and the first of these is illustrated *(Fig 56.1(b))* alongside an underglaze blue/overglazed red bat sauce dish of similar design and age. The sherd appears to be of a bowl lid and is of infinitely better quality than its neighbour.

Fig 56.1 Underglaze Blue from the Guangxu Period

Fig 56.2 Reverse View (dish dimension 101mm diam)

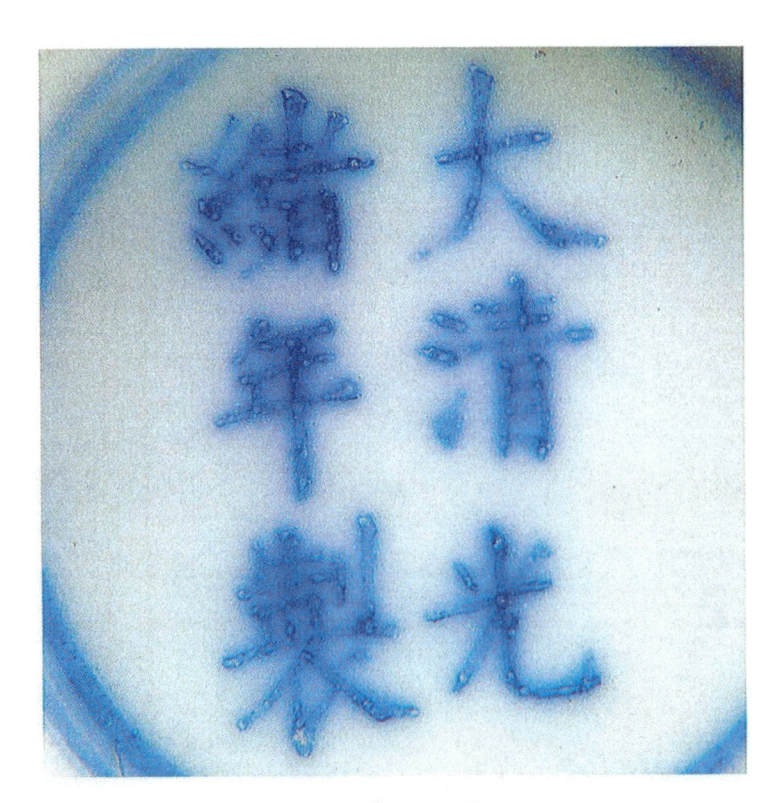

Fig 56.3 Close-up of Mark on Guangxu Sherd

The close-up of the mark *(Fig 56.3)* of this sherd does not show 'countable bubbles' but rather 'split lines', bubble bursts, and distinct variations in the blue colour.

Fig 57.1 Comparison of Late Qing Export with a Modern Fake

	(a)	(b)
Type:	Plate	Spittoon
Design:	Nanking	Butterflies
Dimensions:	190mm diam	180mm diam
Mark:	Made in China	Guangxu (1875-1908)
Dating:	Circa 1891	Circa 1997

The left hand plate *(Fig 57.1(a))* is also a rarity, and I have never seen another similar. Decorated with the late 18th-early 19th Century Nanking pattern, it is from an export dinner service made probably circa 1891, when the US requirement commenced for imported porcelain to be marked with its country of origin. These laboriously hand painted underglaze marks were soon dispensed with for a much faster and easier overglaze iron red stamp.

Fig 57.2 Reverse View

Fig 57.3 Footrim of Guangxu Export Porcelain

Fig 57.4 Footrim of Modern Fake

Fig 57.5 Close-up of Made In China Mark

I first noticed these Guangxu marked spittoons in 1997, when they appeared in a number of dishonest Hong Kong dealers' shops in Hollywood Road and Cat Street.

The immediate give away of a fake is the artificially stained (grey) inside edge to the lid and the footrim.

Fig 58.1 Imperial Monochrome Glazed Porcelains, Guangxu Period

	(a)	(b)
Type:	Vase (Hu)	Vase (Fanghu)
Design:	Teadust	Clare de lune
Dimensions:	325mm H	310mm H
Mark:	Guangxu (1875-1908)	Guangxu (1875-1908)
Dating:	Guangxu	Guangxu

Fig 58.2 Reverse View

The two vases *(Fig 58.1)* are both Guangxu mark and period products of the Imperial factory. The teadust glaze was purportedly reserved for the Emperor, but as there are numerous examples of Qing dynasty pieces without reign marks, this may be dismissed as another Chinese fable. The pale blue 'fanghu' vase (the teadust is 'hu') is of a colour known as 'clair de lune', which in this case changes colour to almost a grey, depending on the position of the light.

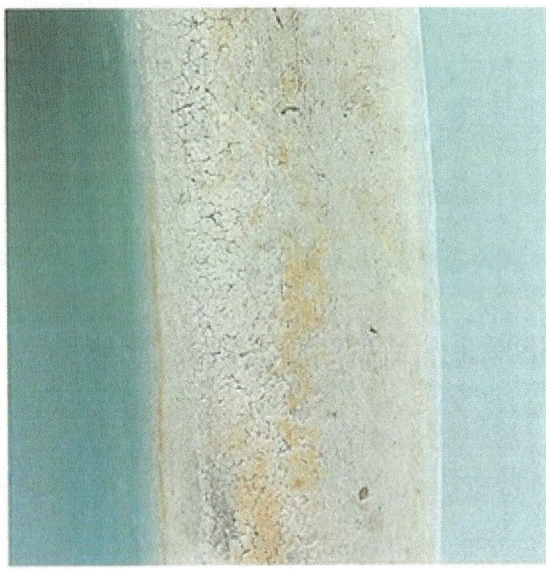

Fig 58.3 Footrim of Fig 58.1(a)

Fig 58.4 Footrim of Fig 58.1(b)

These vases, particularly the teadust, have attracted the attention of the modern day copyist. Fortunately they have difficulty duplicating these pieces, many of which will be immediately detected by their poor quality calligraphy. The teadust mark on this example is incised into a rectangular panel, while the fakes that I have seen to date have an underglaze blue six character kaishu mark; and the underside is not covered in the teadust glaze.

The footrims of *Fig 58.3 & 58.4* are unusual for Guangxu porcelains, having an almost chalk-like coating, suggesting perhaps that a special body formulation was used for these glazes.

Fig 59.1 Yellow Glazed Porcelains of the Guangxu Period

The range of yellow colours of the Guangxu period can be seen in the four examples of *Fig 59.1*. The yellow bowl *(Fig 59.1(b))* and the green and yellow bowl *(Fig 59.1(d))* were in my opinion made for the use of the Imperial household, but I doubt the other two were of sufficient quality to qualify for that purpose. They may, however, have been made in the Imperial factory for commercial sale. Note the anhua (secret) decoration of dragons under the glaze.

Many of these Imperial yellow glazed cups and saucers were very delicately potted, and hairline cracks are a recurring problem for collectors. The cross sectional view *(Fig 60.1)* of a saucer which I carelessly broke, shows a fine white glassy body only 1 to 1.5mm thick.

Fig 60.1 Cross section of Imperial Saucer

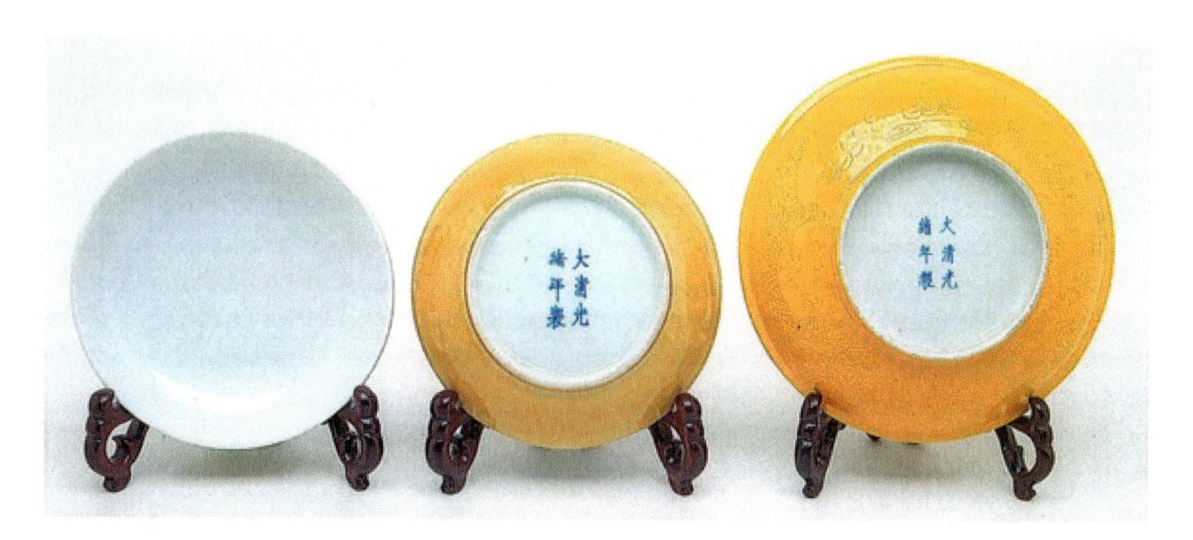

Fig 61.1 Comparison of Guangxu Imperial Yellow with a Modern Fake

	(a) & (b)	(c)
Type:	Small Saucer	Saucer
Design:	Yellow Glaze	Dragons Under a Yellow Glaze
Dimensions:	110mm diam	130mm diam
Mark:	Guangxu (1875-1908)	Guangxu (1875-1908)
Dating:	Guangxu	Modern Circa 1994

The two little saucers *(Fig 61.1(a) & (b))* are rarities from the Guangxu period, because these yellow saucers usually have black or brownish-black marks, not underglaze blue. The yellow outer/white inner, was a colour combination reserved for the first rank concubine, and I suspect these may have been for her personal use.

The neighbouring fake *(Fig 61.1(c))* made circa 1994, is easily distinguishable and copies bearing this glaze with Guangxu mark are not restricted just to saucers, for I have seen small cups and vases also.

Fig 62.1 Comparison of Guangxu Imperial Wine Cup with a Modern Fake

	(a) & (b)	(c)
Type:	Imperial Wine Cup	Imperial Wine Cup
Design:	Iron Red Dragons	Iron Red Dragons
Dimensions:	60mm diam	60mm diam
Mark:	Guangxu (1875-1908)	Guangxu (1875-1908)
Dating:	Guangxu	Modern Circa 1997

As I mentioned earlier, it is my understanding that the modern day Chinese potters cannot duplicate the Qing yellow because of the ban today on firing the potentially lethal antimony which was used as a colouring agent. Having said that, it may have again been used as late as the 1970s, as is evidenced by pieces in the Hong Kong collection of Mrs Barbara Park. Her yellow collection which she kindly allowed me to view, includes reproductions of the Daoguang Imperial yellow, at least of the original quality, distinguishable only by their excessive weight, and absence of bubbles in the glaze over the blue. Mrs Park believes them to be Republic period, and I cannot categorically discount that possibility.

The fake Imperial wine cup of *Fig 62.1(c)* has fooled many experts, and visual comparison with its Guangxu period neighbours reveals only minor deviations from the original.

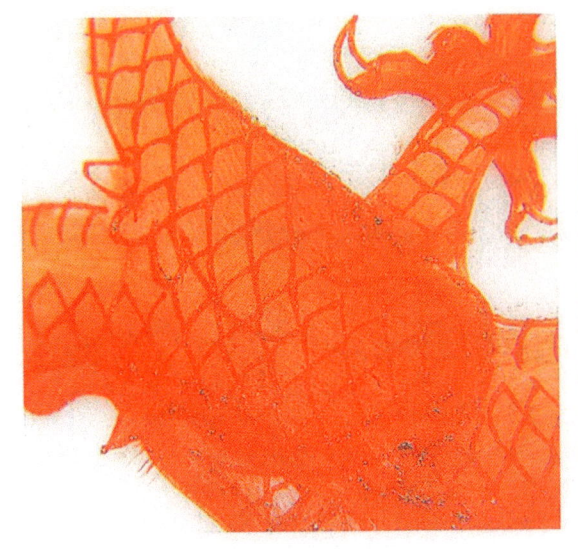

Fig 62.2 Close-up of Guangxu Red Enamel

Fig 62.3 Close-up of Modern Red Enamel

Fig 62.4 Close-up of Guangxu Imperial Mark   *Fig 62.5 Close-up of Fake Guangxu Imperial Mark*

Close-up inspection *(Fig 62.2-62.5)* reveals differences in the manner of drawing the scales, impurities in the earlier iron red, 'split' and 'hollow' lines in the older underglaze blue mark, and 'icing sugar' bubbles in the copy.

These fakes have been mass produced possibly in greater numbers than the original. It should be noted that this design (probably with iron red marks) appears on the Imperial List of 1900, 982 being made in that year for ceremonial use.

Fig 63.1 Enamel Decorated Bowls of the Guangxu Period

	(a)	(b)
Type:	Bowl	Bowl
Design:	Dragons on a Yellow Ground	Aubergine Dragons on a Green Ground
Dimensions:	150mm diam	155mm diam
Mark:	Guangxu (1875-1908)	Guangxu (1875-1908)
Dating:	Guangxu	Guangxu

107

The two bowls of *Fig 63.1* are both unusual and while there is another example in the Victoria & Albert Museum collection, the aubergine dragon design on a green ground is a rarity. Professor van Oort recorded (p 57) that bluish-green and purplish-blue bowls were made for the Guangxu Emperor's wedding in 1889. This bowl is of a quality to have been used for that purpose.

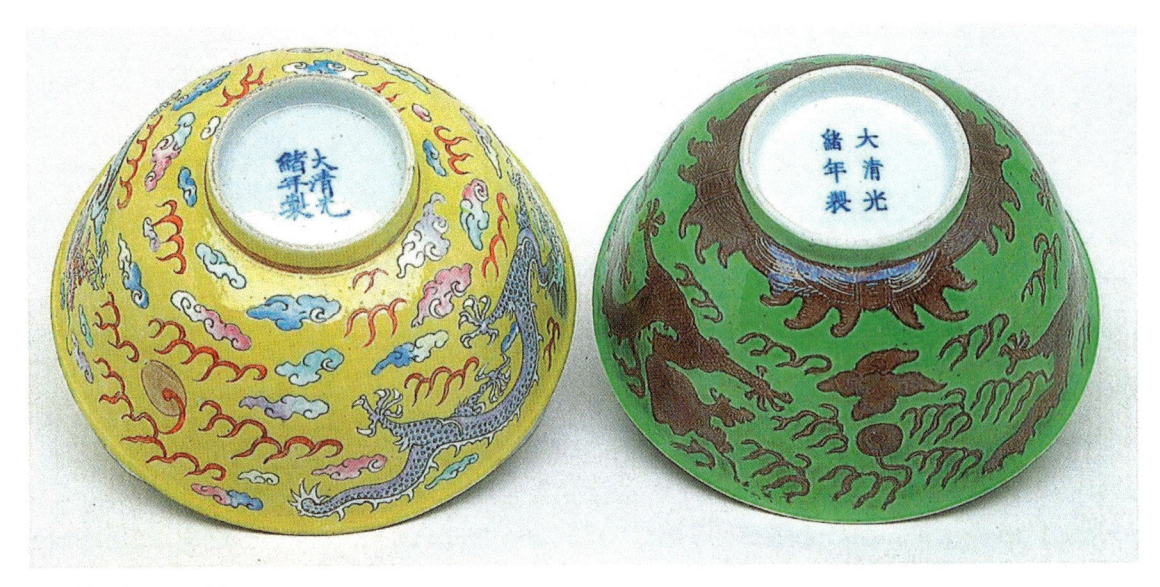

Fig 63.2 Reverse View

Fig 64.1 A Matched Service in the Guangxu 'Birthday' Pattern

The yellow ground porcelains, all with six character kaishu iron red Guangxu marks, illustrated *Fig 64.1*, are from a 'matched' part tea service, decorated in the popular 'birthday' pattern. The reverse view and close-ups of the footrims and enamels show the range of possible variants, all genuine, just from this small selection.

Fig 64.2 Reverse View of Four 'Birthday' Porcelains

Fig 64.3 Footrim of Fig 64.2(b)

Fig 64.4 Footrim of Fig 64.2(c)

Fig 64.5 Footrim of Fig 64.2(d)

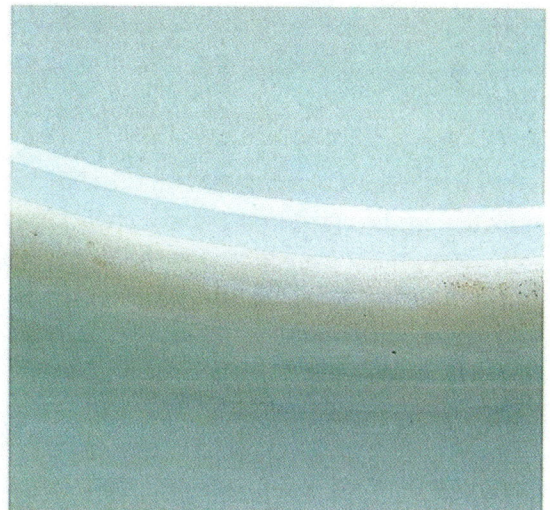

Fig 64.6 Footrim of Fig 64.2(a)

Fig 64.7 Enamel of Fig 64.2(b)

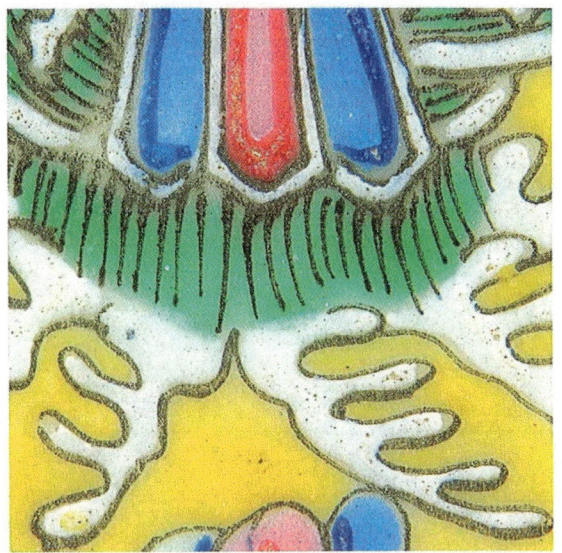

Fig 64.8 Enamel of Fig 64.2(c)

Fig 64.9 Enamel of Fig 64.2(d)

Fig 64.10 Enamel of Fig 64.2(a)

Note the defects in the enamels on all but the last example. Collectors should note that this design is very popular and expensive in Hong Kong and China, but for the moment, relatively inexpensive in most Western countries, the USA excepted.

Plaques or panels of the type illustrated *(Fig 65.1)* are relatively common, and many bear a dated inscription, which as we have seen earlier, may not be contemporary with the date of porcelain manufacture. Dated 1896 and 1889 respectively, these two in my view are probably of the Guangxu period. The studio lighting has exaggerated the stippled 'orange peel' glaze of the round example.

Many of these older plaques were fired back to back, to reduce buckling in the kiln, and then sawn apart later. They were used sometimes as table screens or for insert into table tops and chair backs.

Fig 65.1 Dated Plaques from the Guangxu Period

	(a)	(b)
Type:	Round Plaque (Panel)	Rectangular Plaque (Panel)
Design:	Figures under a Tree	Mountain Lake
Dimensions:	280mm diam	345mm L x 146mm W
Mark:	None	None
Inscription:	Dated 1896	Dated 1889

Fig 66.1 Rare Guangxu/CHINA Marked Bowl

Type:	Bowl
Design:	Dragon & Phoenix
Dimensions:	110mm D
Mark:	Guangxu (1875-1908) plus CHINA stamp
Dating:	Guangxu (probably after 1891)

Fig 66.2 Footrim of Fig 66.1

Fig 66.3 Enamel of Fig 66.1

The bowl *(Fig 66.1)* is a rarity, bearing as it does both a Guangxu iron red reign mark and a CHINA stamp. As these CHINA stamps were required to be affixed to porcelains exported to America after 1891, it is reasonable to assume that the bowl was made between 1891 and 1908. However, I cannot be categoric about that because I have seen a CHINA stamp affixed to a bronze which dated from the Ming dynasty; applied after 1891 when it was exported.

Note the finely levigated footrim on this bowl, unusual for the period on 'minyao' wares.

Fig 67.1 Canton Famille Rose - Rose Medallion

	(a)	(b)
Type:	Plate	Bowl
Design:	Rose Medallion	Rose Medallion
Dimensions:	245mm diam	117mm diam
Mark:	None	Made in China
Dating:	Circa 1870	Circa 1910-1930
Collection:	Geoffrey C Perkins	

The illustration of the plate and bowl *(Fig 67.1)* will hopefully enable me to clear up a few commonly held misconceptions. Firstly, the specific design here is 'rose medallion', though this style of enamel decoration is commonly known as 'Canton famille rose'; the decoration having been applied in Canton (Guangzhou).

The usual decoration is characterised by a circular medallion and panels, as in this case, alternating between figural and floral scenes. There are numerous variants, but if there is no circular medallion, and no rose sprays, then it is not 'rose medallion'.

It is unlikely that 'rose medallion' was made before circa 1850, and if there is no mark on the back, then the pieces may generally be dateable to the period 1850-1891. Readers should note that most of the American authors on this subject, Feller excepted, have dated this porcelain too early in the 19th Century. The reverse view of the plate *(Fig 67.2)* shows the grey/white body and sandy grit adhesions which are a feature of the Tongzhi and early Guangxu periods, suggesting to me a date of manufacture circa 1870 or a little later.

Fig 67.2 Reverse View

The two rose medallion pieces side by side show clearly the difference in quality, most noticeable after 1891 when the 'China' or 'Made in China' mark became mandatory. Readers should also note that just because a piece has a 'Made in China' (or 'China') mark, it cannot be assumed that it was made in 1891. This bowl in my opinion was made circa 1910, perhaps even as late as 1930, judging by the purity of the enamels in *Fig 67.4*.

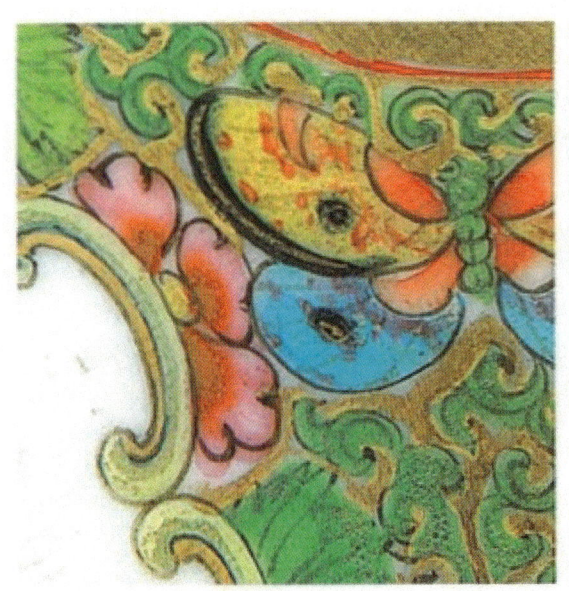

Fig 67.3 Enamels of Fig 67.1(a)   *Fig 67.4 Enamels of Fig 67.1(b)*

Fig 68.1 Floral Decoration of the Guangxu Period

	(a) Top	(b)	(c)
Type:	Plate	Plate	Plate
Design:	Red Ground Sgraffitto	Black Ground Sgraffitto	Green Ground Millefiore
Dimensions:	230mm diam	190mm diam	178mm diam
Mark:	Guangxu (1875-1908)	Guangxu (1875-1908)	Guangxu (1875-1908)
Dating:	Guangxu	Guangxu	Guangxu
Collection:			Geoffrey C Perkins

The three enamelled plates *(Fig 68.1)* show the range of colours available in the Guangxu period, with a slightly whiter, but still grey, glaze and usually without the grit adhesions which so dogged the earlier Tongzhi domestic porcelains. I say usually, because grit adhesions still occurred in the Guangxu reign, but not to the same extent as earlier.

Fig 68.2 Reverse View

Readers may like to compare the black ground plate *(Fig 68.1(b))* with Fig 111 in my earlier book, and then compare these with Fig 279 in Mudge's *"Chinese Export Porcelain in North America"*. Mudge confusingly states the example illustrated by her, from the Peabody Museum collection, to be both Qianlong period and mark, and circa 1835-50. It is in my opinion neither, probably dating to the very late Qing (1900-1912) or early Republic (after 1912).

Examination of the three enamel close-ups show the expected defects, pinholing, opacity and wear one should expect from this period. Compare the enamels of the rose medallion bowl of *Fig 67.4*, and readers will see why I suggested a circa 1910-1930 dating for that piece.

Fig 68.3 Enamels of Fig 68.1(a)

Fig 68.4 Enamels of Fig 68.1(b)

It was a popular custom to mark the Emperor's reign name on spoons in the Guangxu reign, as these mark and period examples *(Fig 69.1)* illustrate. Note the spur marks in the glaze of the underside where the spoon was elevated clear of the saggar.

Fig 68.5 Enamels of Fig 68.1(c)

Fig 69.1 Spoons of the Guangxu Period (Av. 145mm L)

Fig 70.1 Enamel Decoration of the Guangxu Period

All of the pieces illustrated *(Fig 70.1)* are Guangxu mark and period, showing again the diversity of enamel decoration in the late 19th and early 20th Century. The left hand cup bears a relatively rare Guangxu seal mark in place of the more usual kaishu mark. The rear butterfly saucer was part of a larger service, whence came one of the spoons last illustrated, as was the small *doucai* cup in the centre front.

Fig 70.2 Reverse View

Fig 71.1 A Guangxu Mark & Period Enamelled Plate

Type: Plate
Design: Buddhist Symbols
Dimensions: 259mm diam
Mark: Guangxu (1875-1908)
Dating: Guangxu

Fig 71.2 Reverse View

The beautifully decorated but non-Imperial plate *(Fig 71.1)* is unusual for the underglaze blue Guangxu reign mark, with enamel decoration.

Towards the end of the Qing dynasty, and especially in the early Republic period, many decorators used custom-made blanks bought from other potters. Whether this was such a piece we will never know but the underglaze blue mark, in the absence of any other underglaze blue decoration, suggests that it might have been.

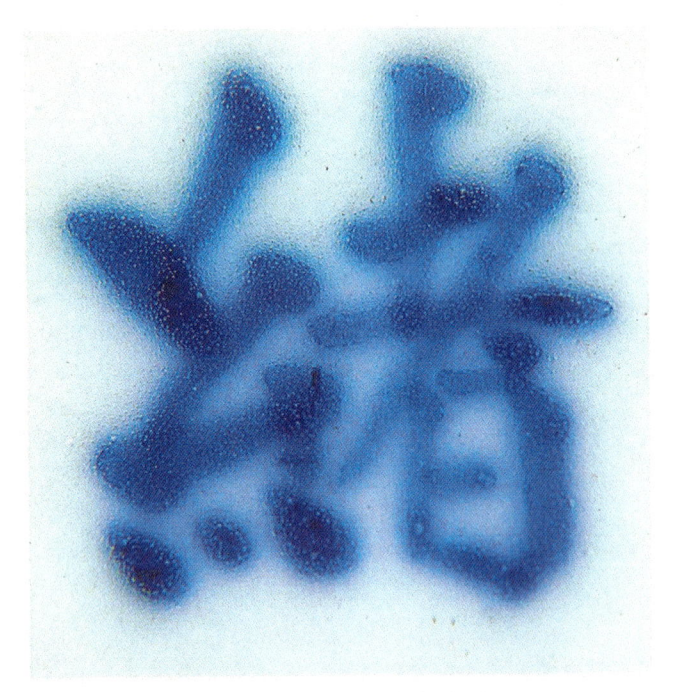

Fig 71.3 Close-up of Xu character of Fig 71.1

Note the misfired iron red rim decoration on the condiment rim (6 o'clock) of this plate. The bubbles in the glaze above this mark *(Fig 71.3)* are so fine that if it was not for the other features which distinguish this piece as late Qing it could, by the mark alone, have been mistaken as a modern copy.

However, the imperfections in the enamels, the grey/white glaze on the back, the white/pink enamel, coarse footrim, and typical reverse decoration, all point to a dating contemporary with the mark.

The large dish *(Fig 72.1)* is an unusual survivor of this period, bearing an iron red six character Guangxu reign mark.

The reverse view *(Fig 72.2)* and close-up of the footrim *(Fig 72.3)*, show the coarse body which is a feature of so many of the larger items from the late Qing; platters, vases, jars, etc. The underside is a distinct grey, not the bluish tinge that *Fig 72.3* shows. Note again, the imperfections in the enamelling *(Fig 72.4)*.

Fig 72.1 Large Dish -
 Guangxu Mark
 & Period

Type: Large Dish
Design: Bird in a Branch
Dimensions: 360mm diam
Mark: Guangxu
 (1875-1908)
Dating: Guangxu

Fig 72.2 Reverse View

Fig 72.3 Footrim of Fig 72.1   *Fig 72.4 Enamel of Fig 72.1*

One of the intriguing aspects of collecting Chinese porcelain from a financial perspective has been the relative lack of importance placed on the time taken to complete the piece originally. Take the lidded vase of *Fig 73.1*, which although exquisitely decorated and would have taken the artist several days to complete, until only recently could have been purchased for perhaps $US150. The adjoining ginger jar is from the same factory.

Fig 73.1 Further Enamels of the Late Qing (Rooster 225mmH)

The pair of 'splash glazed' biscuit-decorated green, yellow, aubergine and blue roosters, and the saucer, were made in China somewhere other than Jingdezhen. The glazed back of the saucer is so crazed that it looks like a piece of Japanese Satsuma pottery, a factor which has confused generations of collectors since their manufacture in the late Qing dynasty.

Fig 73.2 Reverse View

Fig 73.3 Footrim of Fig 73.1(b)

Fig 73.4 Enamel of Fig 73.1(b)

Fig 73.5 Glaze of Fig 73.1(a)   *Fig 73.6 Glaze of Fig 73.1(c) (saucer)*

These green, yellow and aubergine porcelains (and the rooster with the added blue) were decorated on the biscuit (ie: the colours were not applied to a preglazed body), and are commonly known as 'egg and spinach' glazes. They are of the same family of ceramic figures as the joss stick holder illustrated in my earlier book *(Fig 5)*.

Fig 74.1 Enamelled Porcelains of the late Qing

	(a)	(b)	(c)
Type:	Mug	Plate	Bowl
Design:	Pekinese Dogs	Contending Dragons	Quail Among Rocks
Dimensions:	95mmH	240mm diam	138mm diam
Mark:	Guangxu (1875-1908)	None	Guangxu (1875-1908)
Inscription:	Autumn 1908	None	1923
Dating:	Guangxu	1865-1880	Guangxu

124

The design of iron red and green enamel Pekinese dogs was a popular design around 1900 *(Fig 74.1(a))* and appears on large vases and lidded jars in substantial numbers. This mug bears not only a Guangxu four character seal mark on the base but a dated inscription to Autumn 1908.

On reflection, the green and black dragon plate *(Fig 74.1(b))* is misplaced in this chapter as in my view, it more correctly dates to the Tongzhi/early Guangxu era, circa 1865-1880. The method of drawing the dragon's scales individually is unusual for this period.

The bowl *(Fig 74.1(c))* has been a matter of some discussion and argument as to its dating. It bears a Guangxu six character iron red reign mark which appears to be contemporary with the enamels and potting. The dated inscription has been translated variously as 1903 (by one of Singapore's foremost experts), and 1923 by a senior Chinese/New Zealand translator.

The 1923 dating seems to be correct, suggesting that the inscription must have been added at least 15 years after the other decoration was applied. Some dealers believe that after the collapse of the Qing dynasty, some early Republic potters continued to apply Qing reign marks.

While I cannot rule out this possibility, it is pieces like this bowl which tend to support such theories.

Fig 74.2 Reverse View

Fig 74.3 Guangxu Seal Mark of Fig 74.1(a)

Fig 74.4 Footrim of Fig 74.1(a)

Fig 74.5 Guangxu Mark of Fig 74.1(c)

Fig 74.6 Enamels of Fig 74.1(c)

Fig 75.1 Snuff Bottles Old and New

	(a)	(b)
Type:	Snuff Bottle	Snuff Bottle
Design:	Boating Scene	Dragons and Figures
Dimensions:	72mmH	80mmH
Mark:	Leaf	Guangxu
Dating:	Circa 1900-1915	Circa 1997

Fig 75.2 Reverse View

Snuff bottles continue to be made up until today, but most of the older ones will be identified by the features which I have discussed earlier. The underglaze blue example *(Fig 75.1(a))* is dateable circa 1900 from its footrim, but the thin blue decoration suggests a slightly later date; perhaps even early Republic.

The neighbouring enamelled snuff bottle, by comparison, has a rough footrim; unusual for new pieces. The enamels are thick and relatively constant in colour, without the imperfections which may be seen, for example, in *Fig 68.3* to *68.5*. Note also the strange purply blue and bright orange, colours which if they were made in the late Qing dynasty, I cannot recall having seen applied in this colour combination.

Fig 75.3 Underglaze Blue of Fig 75.1(a) *Fig 75.4 Modern Day Enamels*

It is worthwhile to comment again at this stage on the application of apocryphal reign marks, for many errors in dating would be averted, if collectors and dealers appreciated that a Yongzheng or Qianlong or Jiaqing mark (and in most cases, Kangxi too) when not of the period, signifies a date later than 1865; and in most cases, after 1910. Bushell, writing circa 1895 (p 159) wrote:

> *"A visit to the commonest crockery shop in China will confirm this; the blue and white pieces will generally be found marked Xuande (Hsuan Te), and those enamelled in colours, Chenghua (Ch'eng Hua) ..., the larger vases and jars provided for wedding presents will probably have seals of the reigns of Kangxi (Kang Hsi) or Qianlong (Chien Lung) inscribed underneath; as the shops are not kept by curio dealers, nobody is taken in; it is simply a custom of the trade."*

The beautiful celadon ground vase *(Fig 76.1)* is such an example, bearing a Qianlong (1736-1795) 'reversed S' mark, but in my view, made a little later than Bushell's commentary, circa 1910-1915.

My good friend Mr Tai observed that both the shape and the enamelling suggested perhaps even an early Republic (after 1912) dating, but in order that I do not rule out a late Qing dating, I have suggested circa 1910-1915. Certainly the underglaze blue colour in my view appears to be the imported cobalt; and if the Chinese historical records are correct, then this must have been made after 1910.

The beauty of the celadon glaze and the enamelling is in sharp contrast to the roughly levigated and poorly finished underside. A rounded octagon must have been an extremely difficult shape to produce, and I have been unable to find this shape made in the Qianlong reign. Perhaps, like today's fakesters, this potter thought that a unique shape and design was less likely to be detected than a fake of an original?

Fig 76.1 Octagonal Vase - Circa 1910

Type:	Large Vase
Design:	Celadon Ground
Dimensions:	525mmH
Mark:	Qianlong (1736-1795)
Dating:	Circa 1910-1915

Fig 76.2 Reverse View

Fig 76.3 Footrim of Fig 76.1

Fig 76.4 Enamels of Fig 76.1

130

Fig 76.5 Qianlong Mark, Fig 76.1

Fig 77.1 Modern Day Fakes Bearing Guangxu Marks

Fig 77.2 Reverse View

The porcelain pieces illustrated *(Fig 77.1)* all bear Guangxu reign marks, but all are modern copies. The best, and most difficult to detect is the yellow magpie bowl; the most noticeable defects being a complete absence of wear and the orange tinge to the yellow enamel *(Fig 77.6)*. The footrim and glaze *(Fig 77.5)* could otherwise have come from a Guangxu original.

The lavender dish, without the 'antique reproduction label', would fool many experienced dealers, but the gritty footrim is too regular to have been made in the Guangxu period; and the excessively bubbly glaze *(Fig 77.4)* is just not contemporary with a Guangxu dating.

The iron red enamel used by today's fakester is virtually devoid of other debris, and the darker spots *(Fig 77.7)* are only enamel accumulations at the end of a stroke.

Similarly with the bats on the red enamelled and gilded bowl. Compare these with the iron red say of *Fig 74.5* and the genuine Guangxu debris will be seen scattered through the strokes, not just at the ends.

Fig 77.3 Footrim of Fig 77.2(b)

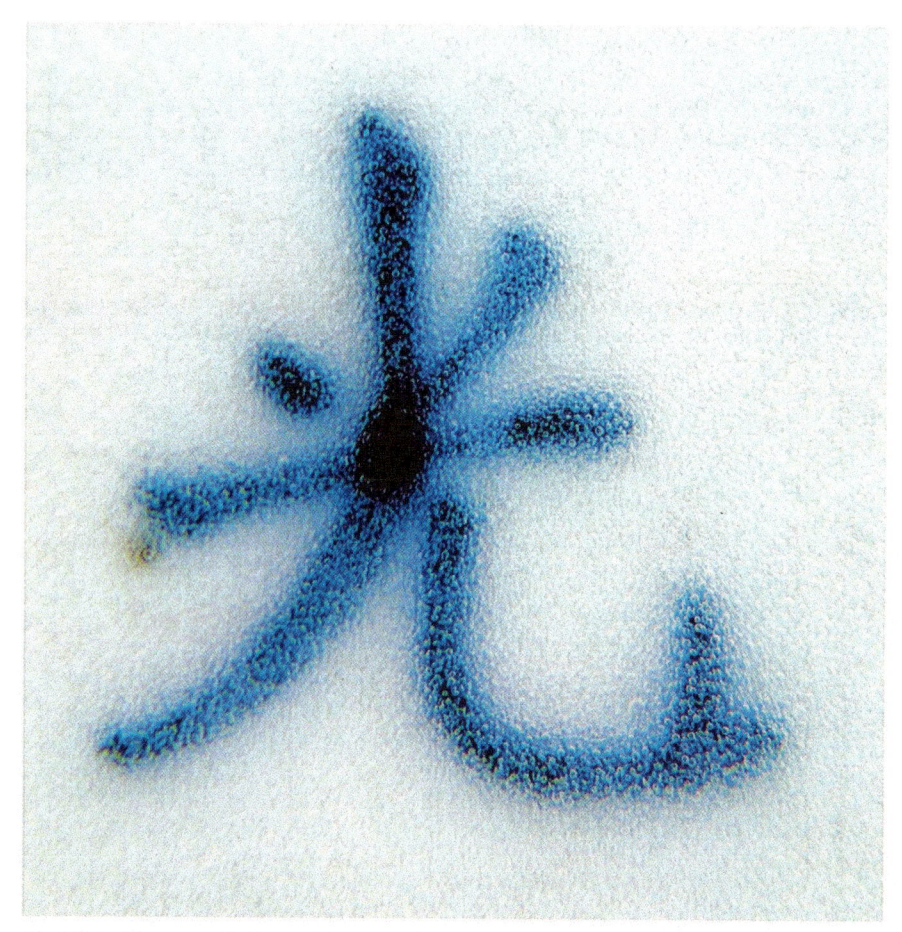

Fig 77.4 Close-up of Guang Character, Fig 77.2(b)

Fig 77.5 Footrim of Fig 77.1(a)

Fig 77.6 Enamels of Fig 77.1(a)

133

Fig 77.7 Mark of Fig 77.1(a)

Fig 77.8 Bats of Fig 77.1(e)

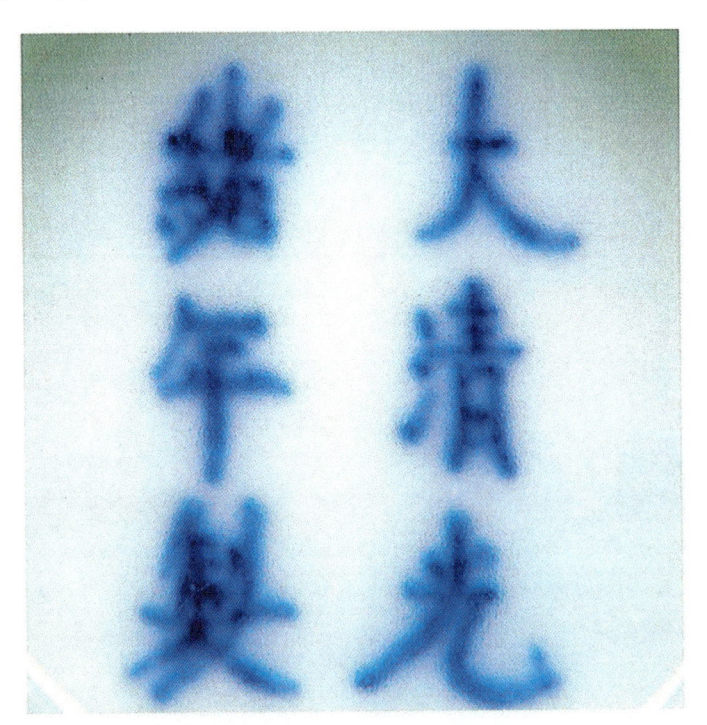

Fig 77.9 Modern Guangxu Mark from Fig 77.1(d)

The close-up of the mark *(Fig 77.9)*, taken from the little green wine cup, shows a distinct contrast in bubble definition compared with *Fig 77.4*. These again are the 'icing sugar' bubbles and constant blue hue which are frequent features of the modern imitations.

CHAPTER SEVEN
XUANTONG REIGN
(1909-1912)

The last Emperor to the Qing throne, Puyi, reigned via a regency from 1909 until his abdication on 12 February 1912. His reign was known as Xuantong. Readers should note that because the Chinese year commences with the Chinese New Year, most books refer to his reign ceasing in 1911.

Xuantong mark and period porcelains are highly collectible, as astute collectors have noted the shortness of his reign and concentrated on it. They are now scarce and becoming increasingly expensive.

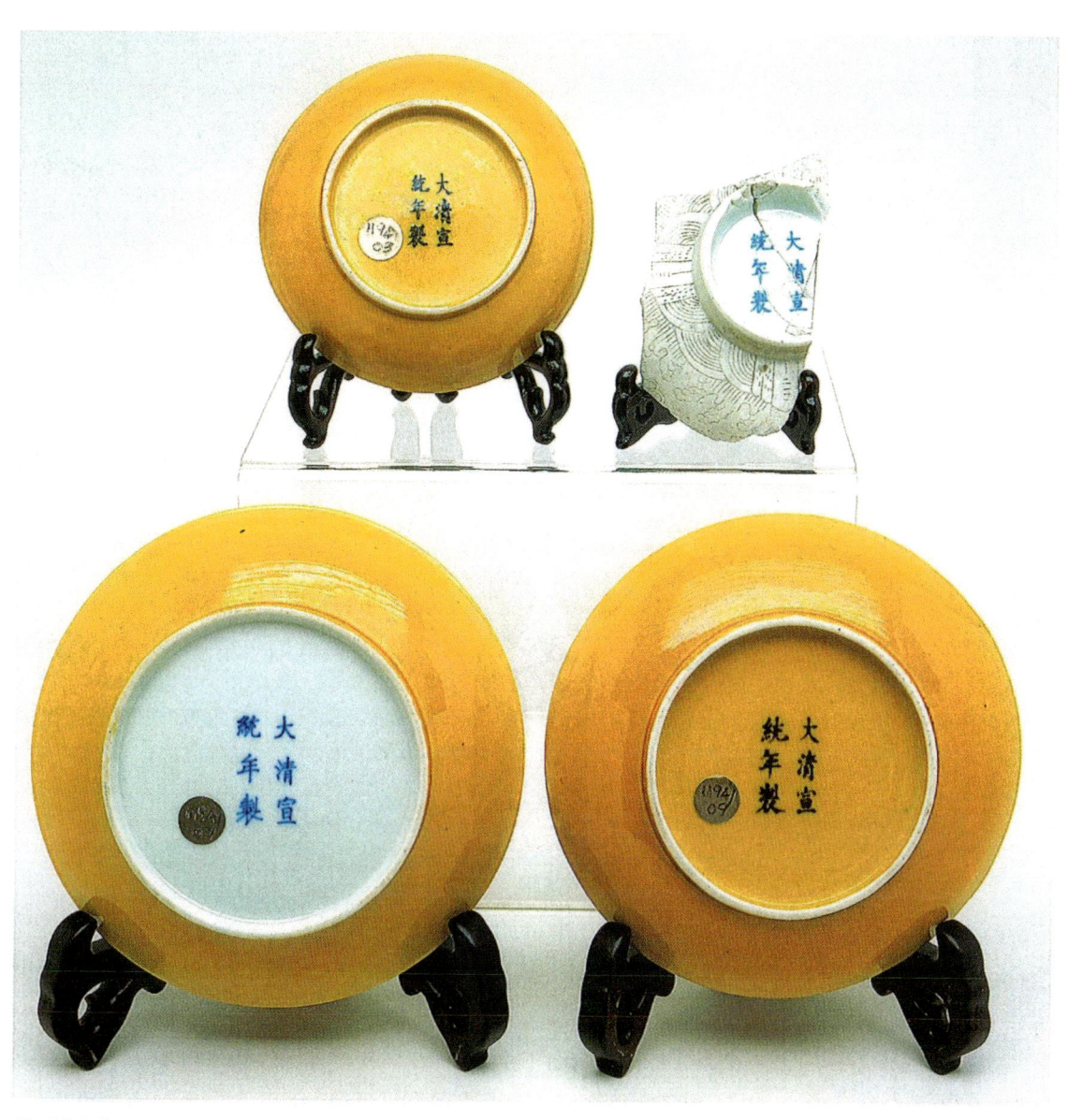

Fig 78.1 Imperial Porcelains of the Xuantong Period

I was very fortunate, on my visit to Jingdezhen, to acquire a discarded Xuantong sherd from the Imperial factory. This sherd provides us with the opportunity to see the 'anhua' (secret) decoration, before glazing. The three neighbouring Imperial yellow saucers, all bearing Xuantong reign marks, show the iridescent glaze which identifies these from many modern reproductions.

Fig 78.2 Footrim of Xuantong Sherd

Fig 78.3 Mark of Fig 78.1(c)

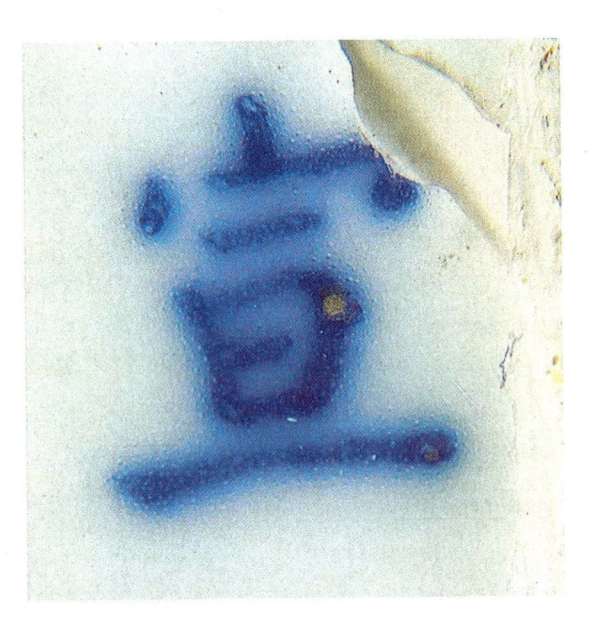

Fig 78.4 Mark of Xuantong Sherd (Fig 78.1(b))

The two Xuantong marks *(Fig 78.3 & 78.4)* have clearly not been written by the same Imperial calligrapher, but note the consistency of the two 'countable bubble' glazes, and again the variations in the density of the blue.

Incidentally, for those readers interested, the white backed yellow saucer *(Fig 78.1(c))* is 148mm diam, and the front (not shown) is yellow. Further research needs to be undertaken to establish whether or not these white backed pieces were for the Imperial household (Emperor, Empress and Empress Dowager), as I suspect, while the brown/black marked pieces were for ceremonial use in the Temple of the Earth.

Fig 79.1 Wine Cup Warmer dated 1909

Type: Wine Cup Warmer
Design: Mountain and Lake Scene
Dimensions: 100mmH
Mark: Dated Inscription to 1909
Dating: Circa 1900-1909

The wine cup warmer is decorated with a style of enameling known to the Chinese as qianjiang. While common usage has included this style of decoration as 'qianjiang', the true 'qianjiang' style copies the Yuan dynasty, which is completed with a reddish-brown colour, inside a design first sketched in ink; and finished with small amounts of other colours, including pale blue, moss green, and aquamarine. A style very popular in the late Qing and early Republic period, this piece bears a dated inscription to 1909; not necessarily its date of manufacture but almost unquestionably the date the inscription was applied.

Fig 79.2 Reverse View

The lidded vase in the famille verte palette *(Fig 80.1)* provides readers with the opportunity to compare a late Qing fake copying the Kangxi period, with the genuine article (of *Fig 12.1*). If there is ever any doubt about the dating of famille verte porcelains, it is usually the poorly levigated footrim that will be the give-away *(Fig 80.3)*. The enamels are often grubby and opaque, and thinly applied in comparison with their Kangxi counterparts which they seek to emulate (see *Fig 80.4*).

Fig 80.1 Famille Verte Enamel Vase

Type: Lidded Vase
Design: Famille Verte
Dimensions: 305mmH
Mark: Double Circle
Dating: Circa 1900-1910
Courtesy: Oliver Watson

Fig 80.2 Reverse View

Fig 80.3 Footrim of Fig 80.1

Fig 80.4 Enamels of Fig 80.1

138

I have illustrated the two bowls of *Fig 81*, largely to remind myself of my own carelessness, for I purchased the right hand Xuantong marked example, believing (but suspicious) that it was genuine. I bought the Guangxu marked piece later in Jingdezhen.

Fig 81.1 Inner View of Fake Guangxu and Xuantong Bowls

Fig 81.2 Reverse View

Fig 81.3 Enamels of Fig 81.1(a)

Fig 81.4 Close-up of Mark of Fig 81.1(b)   *Fig 81.5 Close-up of Xuan Character Fig 81.1(b)*

    Close-up examination of the enamels should have shown the absence of imperfections, and the artificially dirtied footrim is an immediate alert.

    But there are other defects which I should have taken into account; too perfect glazing, large oversized bubbles running in lines, and the strange coloured blue (which I mistook as the Xuantong imported cobalt).

    This is a convenient reminder to readers that even the so-called experts make mistakes; and sometimes, stupid ones at that.

CHAPTER EIGHT
REPUBLIC PERIOD
(1912-1949)

Fig 82.1 Porcelain from the Jiangxi Porcelain Industrial Co

Fig 82.2 Reverse View

At the end of the Qing dynasty, a number of privately operated kilns started manufacturing high quality porcelains, and the best known of these is the Jiangxi Porcelain Industrial Company; reportedly operating from 1910 to 1934. The little 'beaker' shaped wine cups of *Fig 82.1*, all bear the underglaze blue marks of this company, the pair of bird decorated cups having also a dated inscription to 1921. The accompanying sherd also came from the Imperial kiln site in Jingdezhen.

In *Fig 82.3*, I have shown the footrim of the sherd *(Fig 82.1(b)*, and in *Fig 82.4*, another footrim close-up, this time of the larger beaker. I am relatively certain that the Jiangxi Porcelain Industrial Company was responsible for the manufacture of many high quality reproductions of the Yongzheng and Qianlong Imperial porcelains, whose identity may be detected by comparison with the footrim and mark close-ups shown here. Note the very white well levigated footrim, with the pronounced yellow edge, sometimes with a tendency to frit, which will be found with an underglaze blue mark which has distinct 'hollow' and/or 'split' line features, as *Fig 82.4 & 82.5* evidences.

Fig 82.3 Footrim of Sherd of Fig 82.1(d)

I have lost track of the number of Yongzheng marked and allegedly period porcelains I have seen, which have these identical features; especially 'doucai' (dovetailing underglaze blue with overglaze enamels) wares.

Fig 82.4 Base of the Larger Beaker, Fig 82.1(c)

Fig 82.5 Base of Bird Cup of Fig 82.1(b)

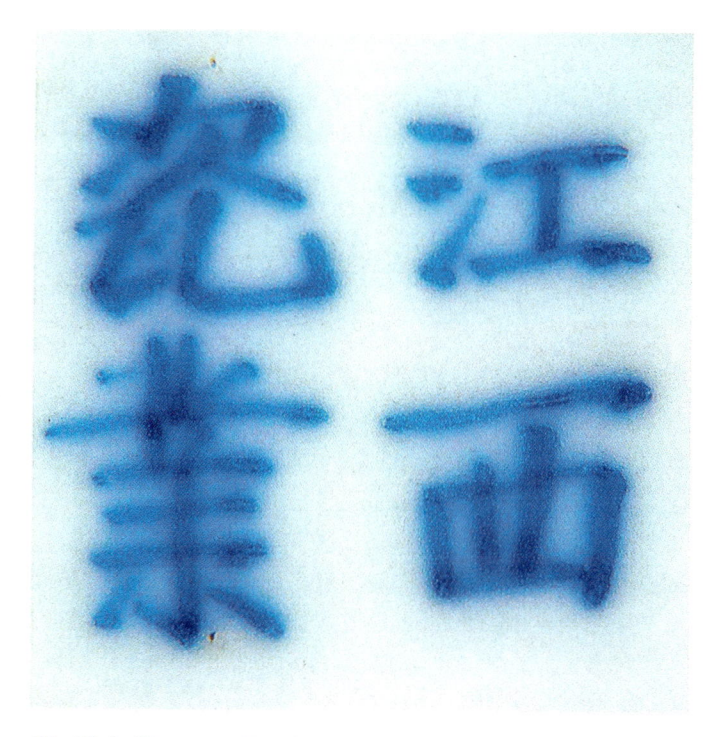

Fig 82.6 Close-up of Mark on Sherd

Fig 83.1 Censers of the Republic Period

Fig 83.1	(a)	(b)
Type:	Censer	Censer
Design:	Dragons	Dragons
Dimensions:	360mmW x 310mmH	365mmW x 310mmH
Mark:	Dated 1926	Dated 1928
Dating:	Circa 1926	Circa 1928

Fig 83.2 Reverse View (inverted)

Censers continued to be ordered and donated to the temples, as the two illustrated *(Fig 83.1)* evidence. Note the difference in the blue colour from the late Qing, and the strange orange and grey bodies on the undersides. These two are dated 1926 and 1928 respectively, their thick bubbly glazes *(Fig 83.3 & 83.4)* almost reminiscent of their Ming predecessors.

I thought initially that the dirt on the surface of the glaze on these censers was from the smoke in the temples, but it defies my efforts to remove it, and seems bedded in the glaze; a somewhat similar defect which I noted on some earlier Kangxi and Qianlong pieces.

Fig 83.3 Date Mark (1926) Fig 83.1(a)   *Fig 83.4 Date Mark (1928) Fig 83.1(b)*

The central brushpot of *Fig 84.1(b)* was purchased from Hong Kong dealer C.Y. Tse, and dated by them to 1900. In my earlier book *(Fig 68(a))*, I suggested a dating of 1910-1915, but my subsequent research suggests a dating of between 1930 to 1940, perhaps even slightly later. It is rare to find two underglaze blue pieces from the Republic period, which have been decorated by the same person and the same calligrapher; as these two brushpots clearly show. Readers should note the glazed footrims and unglazed cream coloured circle on the base of the tall brushpot, a relatively new innovation which appears to have become popular circa 1930; and given the identical phoenix and dragon painting and calligraphy, provides a clue to dating for the central brushpot.

These folded-rim brushwashers *(Fig 84.1(a))* were made in a number of sizes, the larger ones probably used as bulb bowls, and most affixed, not with a Kangxi mark as in this case, but with an apocryphal Qianlong 'reversed S' seal mark.

There is an enamelled seal paste box bearing a dated inscription to 1941, illustrated by Kwan, *"Brush and Clay" (Fig 117)* which has a glazed footrim similar to that of the taller brushpot.

Fig 84.1 Middle Republic Period Underglaze Blue

Fig 84.1	(a)	(b)	(c)
Type:	Brush Washer	Brush Pot	Brush Pot
Design:	Dragon	Dragon and Phoenix	Dragon and Phoenix
Dimensions:	115mmW	75mmH	130mmH x 78mmW
Mark:	Kangxi (1662-1722)	Yongzheng (1723-1735)	Yongzheng (1723-1735)
Dating:	Circa 1930-1940	Circa 1930-1940	Circa 1930-1940

Fig 84.2 Back View

Fig 84.3 Reverse View

Fig 84.4 Close-up of Fake Yongzheng Mark, Fig 84.1(c)

At this point, comment needs to be made about the alleged occupation and/or razing of Jingdezhen, which several authors have referred to; thus leading them to the conclusion that porcelain manufacture ceased. I mention:

147

1. Lim Suan Poh, writing in the excellent SEACS publication "Nonya Ware and Kitchen Ch'ing", (p 29), quotes Malcolm F Farley in a paper read before the Anti-Cobweb Society of Foochow on 20 May 1932 where he stated:
    "Jingdezhen had been completely destroyed 2 years or thereabouts ago when the City fell into the hands of the Communists."

2. Van Oort (p 153) cites:
    "... heavy fighting in Jiangxi in 1927. In 1928, the Red Army entered Jiangxi, but in 1933 was forced out of Jingdezhen, breaking through again in October 1934."

    On page 154, he states that the Japanese took Jingdezhen in 1937.

3. Simon Kwan (*"Brush & Clay"*, p 38/39) stated:
    "Although Jingdezhen itself never fell into Japanese hands, the town was bombed several times by Japanese war planes, and more than 30 kilns were reduced to rubble."

4. Garnsey & Alley (p 113), stated:
    "Jingdezhen was under great duress, enduring almost complete destruction until 1949."

My inquires in Jingdezhen confirmed Kwan's statement that the Japanese never occupied the city, and my own research indicates that despite the civil war and Japanese bombing, porcelain production continued, albeit on a reduced level, right through this period of upheaval.

In this book, I refer readers to the following dated pieces:

Fig 91   Cups dated 1933
Fig 92   Tea pot dated 1933
Fig 93   Table screen dated 1933
Fig 94   Paste box dated 1935
Fig 92   Tile dated 1939
Fig 93   Table screen dated 1944

In addition, Kwan illustrates in *"Brush and Clay"* a number of dated porcelain plaques and vases, with dated inscriptions right through the years 1928 to 1933 and 1937 through 1948.

The most obvious difference between the underglaze blue porcelains of the Republic period and the earlier Qing dynasty, is the colour of the blue; presumably as a result of the change to an imported cobalt circa 1910.

The enamel decorated porcelains of the period in many instances, repeated the designs of the Qing, but in addition, new designs, enamels and styles of decoration were experimented with; some successful, some not.

The two pieces *(Fig 85.1)* bear inscriptions dating to the very early Republic period; 1913 & 1914 respectively. As I stated earlier, readers must be cautious accepting these overglaze inscriptions, as they were often added long after the porcelain had been manufactured. The vase bears an underglaze blue mark reading "Ping Shang Porcelain Co, which I believe operated in Hunan Province   (ie: Not Jingdezhen, Jiangxi Province).

Fig 85.1 Early Republic Enamelled Porcelains
  (a) Dated 1913   *(b) Dated 1914*

Fig 85.2 Back View

Fig 85.3 Reverse View

Fig 85.4 Footrim of Fig 85.1(a)

Fig 85.5 Footrim of Fig 85.1(b)

The footrim of the brushpot is identical to that of the late Qing, a reminder to readers that just because a reign (or dynasty) changed, the porcelain did not necessarily change as well.

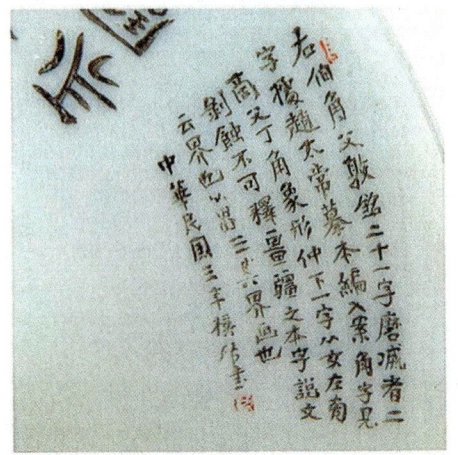

Fig 85.6 Close-up of Calligraphy of Fig 85.1(b)

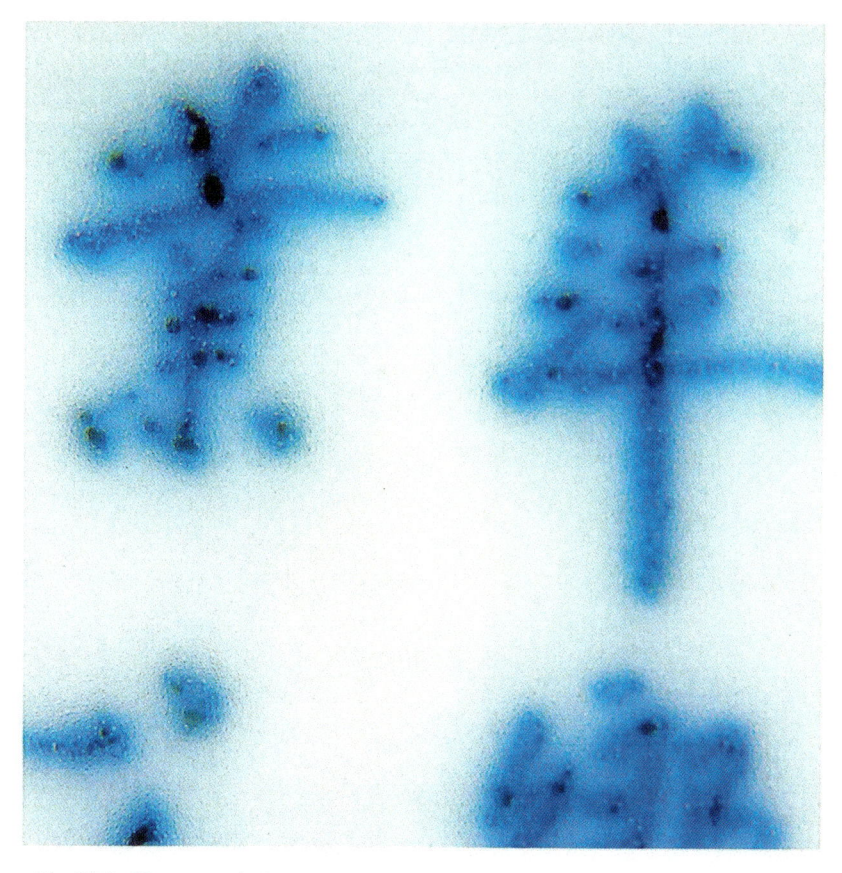

Fig 85.7 Close-up of Ping Shang Mark

For the benefit of interested readers, I illustrate *(Fig 85.7)* a close-up of the Ping Shang Porcelain Co mark. The glaze is noticeably different to that used at Jingdezhen.

Following his abdication and the end of the Qing dynasty, Puyi, the Xuantong Emperor, was permitted to continue to live in residence with his vastly depleted household until 1924. Real power in China after the formation of the Republic lay with Yuan Shikai, who in 1916 proclaimed himself Emperor under the reign name Hongxian, his reign lasting only 83 days.

The Chinese historical records state that the Hongxian Emperor ordered 40,000 pieces of porcelain made for his palace, and there has been considerable controversy in recent years, as to whether or not this quantity was actually made; and if so, what mark was affixed to it.

Professor Van Oort, the first Western writer on these porcelains, concluded that the Hongxian mark was applied to these porcelains during the 83 day reign. His writings provoked much criticism, particularly by Mark Chou, *"A Discourse on Hung Hsien Porcelain"* whose response, in pidgin English, is of dubious merit.

My own belief is that during the period 1912 to 1916, when Yuan Shikai was in residence in a hall named Jurentang, he had porcelain made with the Jurentang mark; as shown on the beautiful presentation vase illustrated *Fig 86.1*.

It is not inconceivable, in fact quite probable, that following his proclamation as Emperor, if 40,000 pieces were ordered, then after 83 days, at least some of the order would have been completed. There are a number of Hongxian marked pieces with dated inscriptions immediately after Hongxian's abdication and subsequent death, giving added support to this proposition.

Fig 86.1 Early Republic Vase   *Fig 86.2 Reverse View*

Type:	Presentation Vase
Design:	Lake and Mountain Scene
Dimensions:	155mmH
Mark:	Jurentang
Dating:	1912-1916

The cancellation of this order must have caused considerable hardship to the potters who were engaged to make it, but they need not have been too worried, because the dispersal of these fine quality porcelains to an admiring population, created much demand; and the Hongxian mark continues to be applied even to this day.

It would have been nice to have tracked the history of this Jurentang marked vase *(Fig 86.1)*, but all I know of it, is that it was found under a house in Christchurch, New Zealand and consigned to auction. The fitted box is contemporary with the suggested date of manufacture of the vase. The fitted box suggests that Yuan Shikai may have had this vase made for presentation as a gift.

Fig 86.3 Jurentang Mark of Fig 86.1

Fig 87.1 Two Early Republic Ceramics (the saucer is modern)

The yixing stone ware bowl *(Fig 87.1(a))* was of course not made at Jingdezhen but it is interesting because it bears a dated inscription to 1921. The neighbouring saucer *(Fig 87.1(b))* is beautifully decorated and marked with a Hongxian seal mark for 1916, but is immediately recognisable as a modern fake by its excessively bright colours, and 'too perfect' glaze. Compare this saucer with the mug dated 1922, which has almost pastel enamels; the predominant palette of the period.

It was quite common in the Republic period for decorators to buy their pre-glazed blanks for decoration; thus giving a diverse range of artists, styles, decorations, and signatures on standard high quality bodies.

Fig 87.2 Reverse View

Whether or not the 1922 date of the inscription is contemporary with the potting, will remain a matter for debate. I suspect that it is, for the porcelains of comparatively roughly finished pieces, like this mug, generally have a better levigated footrim than their late Qing counterparts. This mug was painted by Hong Yishun.

Fig 87.3 Footrim of Fig 87.1(c)

The jardiniere *(Fig 88.1)* bears a mark stating it to have come from the Jiangxi Porcelain Industrial Co, and a dated inscription to 1922 probably added slightly later than the date of manufacture.

Fig 88.1 Jardiniere dated 1922

Type:	Jardiniere
Design:	Lake and Mountain Scene
Dimensions:	245mm diam
Mark:	Jiangxi Porcelain Industrial Company 1922
Dating:	Circa 1922

Fig 88.2 Reverse View

The enamels, to most Western eyes are dull and boring, but these pieces decorated in 'qianjiang-like' enamels, remain popular with Chinese collectors.

The unglazed footrim reveals a body speckled with minute particles of black grit, and the glaze itself has been turned back, presumably after it had dried prior to firing.

In the absence of barely any published research in English on porcelain of the period after 1920, it is difficult to be categoric on the dating of undated porcelains.

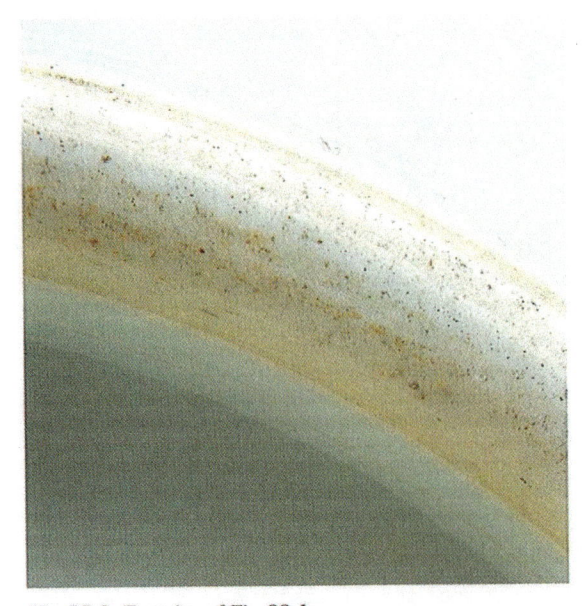

Fig 88.3 Footrim of Fig 88.1

However, the three examples illustrated *(Fig 89.1)* in my opinion are dateable to circa 1930, although the yellow 'shell shaped' brush washer could be slightly earlier. The changeover to the Republic brought with it softer, some would say sombre, enamel colours which would recur again but even to a greater degree, when the Communists took power in 1949.

Fig 89.1 Porcelain of the Mid Republic Period

	(a)	(b)	(c)
Type:	Plate	Vase	Brush Washer
Design:	Yellow Sgraffitto	Lavender Blue Monochrome	Yellow Monochrome
Dimensions:	182mm diam	235mmH	160mmL
Mark:	Jiu Jiang Da Shing Co	Yongzheng (1723-35)	None
Dating:	Circa 1930	Circa 1930	Circa 1920-1930

By around 1925, the colours generally had become brighter, as the yellow sgraffitto ground plate *(Fig 89.1(a))* evidences. Obviously there are exceptions to this rule, but in the main, the artists' palette was dull, in comparison with the Qing. I can find no information on the Jiu Jiang Da Shing Company whose mark appears on the reverse. The lavender blue vase *(Fig 89.1(b))* has a strange 'turned over' lip, which will be found on various shaped vases dating around 1930, in common with the brush washer and larger narcissus bulb bowls which I illustrated earlier *(Fig 84.2(a))*. The close-up of the Yongzheng mark shows an evenly bubbled glaze. Note the artificially blackened rim, which copied the Yongzheng potters which in turn copied the Song. The shell-shaped brushwasher with the delightful frog on the lip, has been glazed with the dangerous antimony yellow (note the iridescence). It is unlikely that this glaze was used much after 1940. There is a strange 'patch' on the inside, visible in the photograph, which does not extend to the outside. Perhaps this was a maker's mark which has been erased?

Fig 89.2 Reverse View

Fig 89.3 Yongzheng Mark of Fig 89.1(b)

Fig 90.1 Enamelled Vase

Fig 90.2 Back View
Circa 1930-1940

The beautifully painted lamp *(Fig 90.1)* would once have been a magnificent vase. Interestingly, it bears a Jurentang mark identical to a pair of vases, illustrated by Kwan (Fig 112) and in his case, signed by Liu Xiren (1906-1967).

Dating between 1930 and 1940, the base glaze and footrim *(Fig 90.3)* show significant improvements, undoubtedly the result of mechanisation in the porcelain industry. The footrim *(Fig 90.4)* is extremely fine and white, without the imperfections of the late Qing.

Fig 90.3 Base and Jurentang Mark of Fig 90.1

The two wine cups *(Fig 91.1)* fooled me and I'm sure will fool others, for they appears to be in colours and design of the late Qing, but bear a dated inscription to October 1932. These cups came from a larger service, all similarly decorated and inscribed. Closer inspection of the enamels reveals 'softer' colours than were used in the Guangxu reign, and while I cannot rule out the possibility that the mark is later than the other decoration, the fact a whole service was similarly decorated, seems to make this possibility unlikely.

Fig 90.4 Footrim of Fig 90.1

Fig 91.1 Wine Cups, dated October 1932

Fig 92.1 'Snow Painting' Porcelain

	(a)	(b)	(c)
Type:	Tea Pot	Tile	Saucer
Design:	Snow	Snow	Snow
Dimensions:	85mmH	72 x 168mm	107mm diam
Mark:	1933	1939 Xu Ren He Yun Painted in Pen Pun (Jiangxi Province)	Qianlong Dated inscription to 1924 (or 1984)
Dating:	Probably circa 1933	Probably circa 1939	Modern circa 1997

From 1930 to 1940, 'snow painting' was popular, the market evidently dominated by an artist named He Xuren. I am in unfamiliar territory here as the style of painting has been much copied; not only in the artist's lifetime, but right up until the present day. As a result of this copying, I have tentatively accepted the dates on the tea pot and tile *(Fig 92.1)*. The saucer, however, was purchased new in Hong Kong in early 1998, but bears a date equivalent to 1924 or 1984.

Fig 92.2 Reverse View

Fig 92.3 Footrim of Tea Pot

The tea pot is dated 1933, made by Yu. Note that the footrim has been glazed.

The tile is dated 1939, marked "Xu Ren He Yun, Painted in Pen Pun" (Jiangxi Province). My translator is adamant that Xu (Xuren) is the surname, not He, as Kwan records on his examples. For the time being, assuming Kwan's pieces are correctly translated, I cannot explain this discrepancy, other than to suggest either:

(a) He (pardon the pun) changed to the Western style of writing, with surname last, or
(b) He did not paint this piece.

Fig 93.1 Table Screen

	(a)	(b)
Type:	Table Screen	Table Screen
Design:	Father and Son Go Fishing	Figures under a Tree
Dimensions:	400mm x 250mm	200mm x 140mm
Mark:	Dated 1933 (by Wang Qi)	Dated 1944
Dating:	Probably a fake (see text)	Circa 1944

The larger table screen *(Fig 93.1(a))* is signed Wang Qi, one of the best known porcelain painters of the Republic period. Wang was born in 1884 and died in 1937, so if this was a genuine work, it would have been at the end of his life. I suspect that it is not his work, although the enamelling appears contemporary with a 1937 date.

The neighbouring table screen is dated 1944, by which time, as *Fig 93.2* shows, the imperfection problems with the enamels had been resolved.

Fig 93.2 Enamels of Fig 93.2(b)

Fig 94.1 Paste Pot, Dated 1934

Type: Paste Pot
Design: Lake and Mountain Scene
Dimensions: 70mm diam
Mark: 23rd Year of the Republic
Dating: Circa 1934

The 1930s were a time of political turmoil (and later, the Japanese occupation) but porcelain production continued, albeit on a reduced scale, as the paste pot dated 1934 evidences *(Fig 94.1)*.

The wall plaque and vase *(Fig 95.1)* show an interesting contrast in decorative techniques, one bright and cheerful, the other sombre and uninviting. Readers must forgive me, but the 'black heart' of Communism had arrived, and with it the dislike for anything colourful or opulent.

I should comment here about the border decoration, because there were subtle changes in the borders, which may provide a clue to dating. I have not shown the 'ruyi pendant' borders of the mid-Republic, starting with a blue enamel around 1930 (perhaps a little earlier), followed by a black enamel in the late 1930s or early 1940s. Ruyi was the head of the ruyi sceptre, and it was sometimes used as a decoration in conjunction with other repetitive Chinese motifs, or as a support for delicate pendants in fine enamelling. Readers should note that both the black and the blue pendant designs continue to be used to the present day, especially on eggshell-like vases.

In the mid to late 1940s, an orange/brown border became popular and was to continue into the 1950s. Note the glazed footrim and unglazed circle which are a feature of the second quarter of the 20th Century. Collectors of tomorrow are going to have a great deal of difficulty in dating many 20th Century porcelains exactly. For whatever little help they are in dating, I have shown close-ups of the enamels and footrims.

Fig 95.1

	(a)	(b)
Type:	Wall Plaque	Vase
Design:	Figures in a Courtyard	Tigers
Dimensions:	217mm diam	170mm H
Mark:	Inscription dated 1946	Inscription dated 1947
		Painted in Zhushan
Dating:	Circa 1946	Circa 1947

Fig 95.2 Footrim of Fig 95.1(a)

Fig 95.3 Enamels of Fig 95.1(a)

165

Fig 95.4 Footrim of Fig 95.1(b)

CHAPTER NINE
MAO PERIOD, PEOPLES REPUBLIC OF CHINA
(1949-1976)

Fig 96.1 Porcelain of the Mao Period

	(a) & (b)	(c)
Type:	Wall Plaques	Lidded Mug
Design:	Lake and Mountain Scene	Tigers
Dimensions:	245mm diam	130mmH
Mark:	Qianlong (1736-1795)	Jiangxi Jing Cheng Art Studio
	Dated Inscription, Summer 1957	Dated 1954
Dating:	Circa 1957	Circa 1954

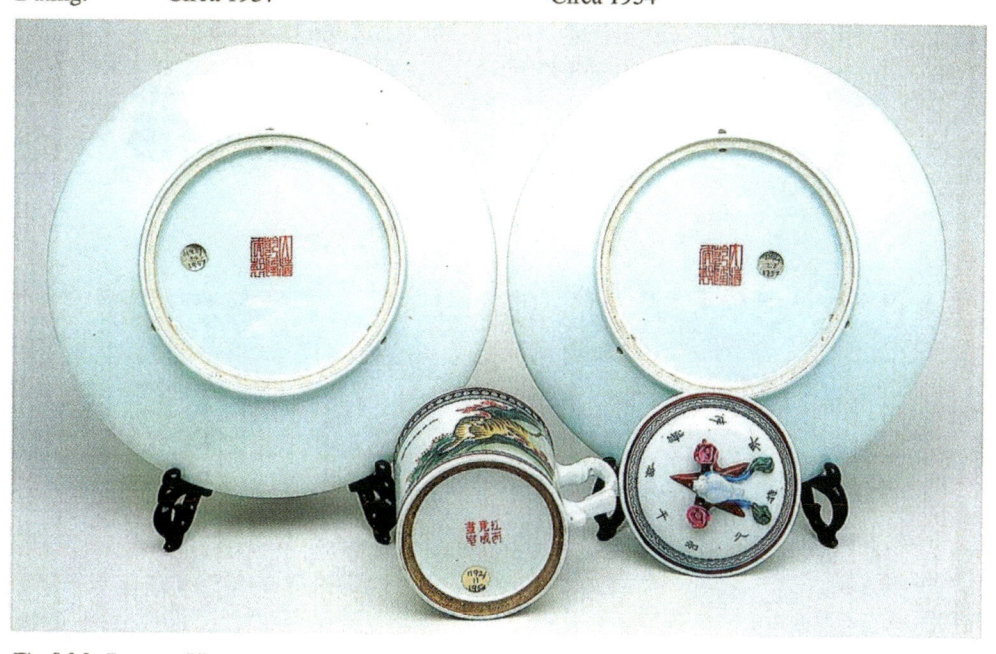

Fig 96.2 Reverse View

167

The wall plaques *(Fig 96.1)* are dated Summer 1957, but a more sombre winter scene would be difficult to depict. Even the trees are drooping.

The lidded mug reflects the Communist propaganda of the Mao period; hammer and sickle handle, an inscription which reads "Lin ... Ling Written 1954 Promote the labour competition, strive hard to win the red flag", and a mark Jiangxi Jing Cheng Art Studio. Curiously, a dove surmounts the lid.

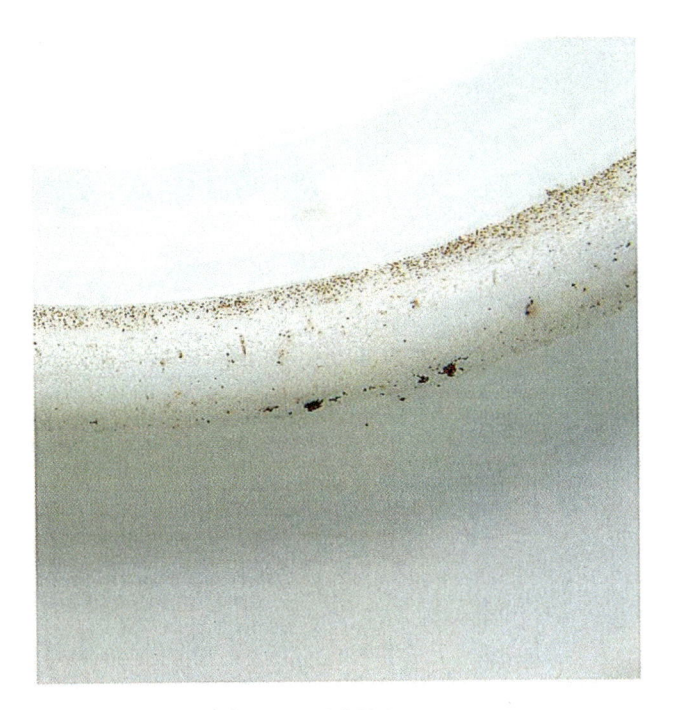

Fig 96.3 Footrim of Lid, Fig 96.1(c)

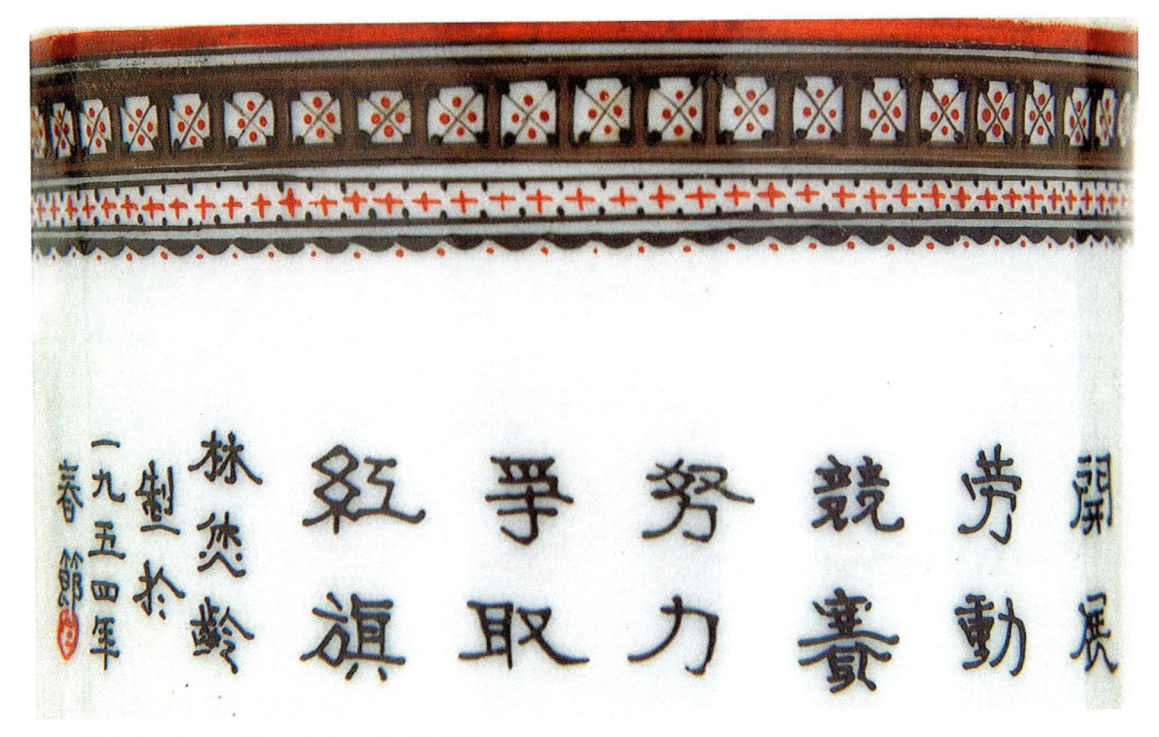

Fig 96.4 Border and Inscription, Fig 96.1(c)

Fig 96.5 Qianlong Mark of Fig 96.1(a)

These wall plaques have a Qianlong reign mark on the reverse, and again the glazed foot and unglazed circle, similar to those shown earlier.

As with most of these inscribed and dated pieces, the inscription was probably added and fired after the porcelain had been made, so the date in most cases will give a finite date of manufacture.

Fig 97.1 Chinese Porcelain of the 1970s and 1980s

	(a)	(b)	(c)
Type:	Bowl	Sauce Dish	Bowl
Design:	Lotus Scroll	Celadon Twin Fish	Lake & Mountain Scene
Dimensions:	115mm diam	100mm diam	125mm diam
Mark:		Longchuan China	Made in China
Dating:	Circa 1974	Circa 1980	Circa 1974
Collection:	Trevor Bayliss		Trevor Bayliss

The two underglaze blue bowls *(Fig 97.1)* were newly acquired by Trevor Bayliss, former curator of applied arts, Auckland War Memorial Museum, on a visit to Jingdezhen in 1974. The little celadon sauce dish, part of a large service, was purchased by an Australian dealer in China in 1980 or 1981. Such details, if not written down, are lost to collectors forever. China had by this date introduced stencil, transfer and stamped designs, which were often complemented by additional hand painting. Stamped designs, of course, had been used on 'minyao' porcelains for centuries.

Fig 97.2 Reverse view

CHAPTER TEN
POST-MAO 20TH CENTURY
(1976-1999)

Fig 98.1 Vase Circa 1998 (200mm H)

Fig 98.2 Same Vase, Lit

Fig 99.1 Modern Day Snuff Bottles, circa 1998

Fig 100.1 Modern Day Artist Signed and Dated Porcelains

There have been numerous new innovations throughout the Post-Mao period, arguably the most important being the development of the 'eggshell' thin porcelains. The vase *(Fig 98.1)* is another example, being plain white in appearance until it is lit from the inside; revealing blue and red secret decoration. I have also seen green.

The traditional shapes and colours remain popular, and the modern day snuff bottles *(Fig 99.1)* will usually be found with an apocryphal Qianlong mark, even though there was probably never an original Qianlong mark and period snuff bottle made with any of these designs or shapes.

Today, it is gratifying to see that the artists are being encouraged to experiment with new shapes, designs and techniques of decoration, despite the pitifully low incomes that all but the most senior ones receive. I took a fancy to the two freely drawn plates *(Fig 100.1)*, on my visit to Jingdezhen in April 1998, and acquired them for 50RMB (about $US6) each.

I also purchased, but from different factories, the superbly decorated vase and teapot of *Fig 101.1 & 102.1*. There can be no question that the modern factories have the ability to duplicate the quality of the best of the 18th Century Imperial porcelains; but not exactly enough to fool the expert, who will note the slightly garish and shiny enamels, the wrong shade of turquoise, and the traditional artificial 'ageing' of the footrim.

Fig 101.1 Modern Day Reproductions of Qianlong Imperial Porcelains

Fig 101.2 Reverse View Showing Qianlong Reign Marks

Fig 102.1 Superb Quality Modern Vase (375mmH)

Top quality large size reproductions, such as those shown in *Fig 102.1*, are seldom seen for sale outside China, the Hong Kong 'antique' dealers usually limiting their stocks to the smaller and less expensive items. In Jingdezhen, the vase cost 1600RMB and the teapot 2000RMB (about $US200 and $US250 respectively). I was to find after a few days that one could buy this quality for around half these prices. For the benefit of posterity, I established the names of the artists involved in decorating this teapot:

The decoration of ladies:	Mao Gui Sheng
The border:	Zhou Shi Tang
The mark:	Tu Sze Zhen

Fig 102.2 Reverse View Showing Qianlong Mark

The owner of the factory where I purchased the vase of *Fig 102.1* (Jingdezhen Jiaying Porcelainware Co Ltd) told me that three men had been engaged on it, and that it took three months to make. One person did the sgraffito and border decoration, another the panels and dog drawings, and another the reign mark.

Fig 102.3 Panels on Fig 102.1

Fig 102.4 Panels on Fig 102.1

The 4800RMB cost ($US600) seemed cheap for a vase of this quality. When I showed it to another manufacturer to show the quality I wanted on an order I was placing, I was told this was not very good quality and I could have bought it for half what I had paid. But this proved to be nonsense when I put it to the test by ordering. My dog vase was equal in quality to the best example of enamelled porcelain available in Jingdezhen in 1998.

Fig 102.5 Panels on Fig 102.1

Fig 102.6 Panels on Fig 102.1

So we end the 20th Century with porcelains being made which equal if not surpass the very best of the 18th Century, some so good that they fool even the world's best authorities. It is now estimated that around five percent of Chinese porcelains appearing in the major auction rooms in Hong Kong are miscatalogued, and an even higher percentage elsewhere.

CHAPTER ELEVEN
A PRELIMINARY LOOK AT THE DATING OF CHINESE REDWARES
(1700AD-2000AD)

When I originally planned the outline of this book, I had intended to intersperse the monochrome red and underglazed red porcelains through the book, in the reign periods where I believed they fitted. By the time I finished the photography, I had accumulated such a range of 'red' porcelains, that I decided to publish a separate chapter on them. To the best of my knowledge, this is the first attempt by a Western author to put some semblance of order into the exceptionally difficult field of Chinese 'redwares'.

I know this chapter will provoke howls of derision from a number of Chinese dealers and academics. I have tried to confirm my own datings, correcting them where necessary, by discussions with several Hong Kong dealers, Mr L H Tai in particular, and with Mr Lei Rui Chun, vice president of the Jingdezhen museum. Neither of these extremely helpful gentlemen, who gave freely of their time and knowledge, can be blamed for whatever errors I will be found to have made.

We know from dated dishes in several major collections that at least one private kiln had mastered the art of underglaze red decoration, by the early to mid. 1670s. The Official Kiln had not commenced production until 1680, so for the time being at least, it will remain a matter of debate as to just when in the Kangxi reign (1662-1722) the Official Kilns commenced making underglaze red decorated wares.

For the past 300 years, Chinese potters have on several occasions mastered and then lost the art of firing underglaze red and their best results were often just 'flukes' of the kiln firing.

The Chinese know the different glazes by various names, some of the better known translating as 'sang de boeuf' (ox blood), donkey liver, horse's lung, sacrificial red, fresh red, peach blossom, peachbloom, flambe, and *jun* red.

With the exception perhaps of saucer dishes in sacrificial red glaze (or badly damaged examples), all of these red colours if made before 1865 are now rare and consequently expensive to purchase; beyond the 'purse strings' of all but the most wealthy collectors. So I have concentrated, with the exception of the 'peachblooms' and the sacrificial reds, on the more available red glazes, which in the main date from the fourth quarter of the 19th Century.

Circa 1700, the Imperial Kiln mastered the exceptionally difficult technique of firing 'peachblooms', ideally, to quote Bushell, a colour *"pale red becoming pink in some parts, in other mottled with russet spots, displayed upon a background of light green celadon tint"*.

There are a number of misconceptions about the 'peachblooms', which I believe are worth correcting. Firstly, they were first made in the Kangxi period, but were not necessarily marked with the Imperial reign mark (ie: Bushell, for example, shows unmarked Kangxi period peachblooms). Secondly, those that were marked with the Kangxi reign mark, appear to have only been made in one of eight different forms.

Thirdly, some Chinese experts believe that peachblooms were only made in the Kangxi and Guangxu reigns. If one accepts the Western definition of a 'peachbloom', this is not correct, for they were made also in Yongzheng and Qianlong, and to my knowledge not by the Imperial factory in the Guangxu period. Readers who can also read Chinese may like to compare Geng Baochang's comments (National Palace Museum) *"Appraisal of Ming and Ching Porcelain"* with those of Bushell.

In the latter half of the 19th Century, 'peachblooms' achieved astronomic prices, as much as $US50,000 in America, causing Hobson to observe in 1915 *"... most of the fine peach blooms have found their way to the United States, and choice examples are rare in England"*. The same is true of China, for as a consequence, there are very few quality peachblooms remaining, and some that are catalogued as Kangxi period are in fact later reproductions.

Over the past five years, I have been studying Kangxi mark and period peachblooms at every opportunity when they appear at auction or for sale; and of the 17 pieces that I have studied, nine have in my opinion been later copies.

This is not a new development, for Hobson in 1915 earlier noted *"that there are exceedingly clever modern copies of the old peach blooms in the market; otherwise how could an inexpert collector in China bring home half a dozen peachblooms bought at bargain prices"*.

It is pertinent to note that all of the nine fakes that I have recently seen were in perfect condition, and my observations have given rise to a personal theory which I will now relate. I believe that an enterprising Chinese in the 19th Century, attempting to capitalise on the very high prices being obtained for peachblooms, accessed either a store of reject porcelain in the Imperial factory (perhaps during the Taiping occupation) or alternatively, and perhaps more likely, ravaged the old Imperial Kiln site for rejects. The reason that I suggest this possibility is that the vast majority of genuine peachblooms in Western ownership show damage or restoration, and many have been restored or embellished with mounts etc at an early date. Interested readers may like to see the numbers of damaged Kangxi peachblooms illustrated by Bushell, circa 1890. The Victoria and Albert Museum beehive-shaped brush washer has been cut down, and the Percival David Foundation's example appears to have been chipped.

I am fortunate to have owned two Kangxi period examples *(Fig 103.1)* also damaged and restored, which while not in the desired peachbloom colour, were intended to be. These two were, like most of the other damaged examples, probably deliberately broken because they failed to meet the exacting requirements of the Kangxi palace.

The interior of the left hand brush washer *(Fig 103.1(a))* has been lined with an ink well, stamped 'silver', probably indicating an American alteration. However, the exterior of the lower rim shows signs that it had been mounted, and the cloisonné rim and jade top, suggests that before American modification, this piece had previously been adapted by the Chinese; maybe just as a lidded brush pot.

The neighbouring brush washer *(Fig 103.1(b))* has had its broken rim crudely restored in metal.

The illustration of the undersides *(Fig 103.2)* provides the opportunity to again quote Hobson:

> *"In every case the bottom of the vessel shows a fine white-glazed porcelain with unctuous paste, and the Kangxi (K'ang Hsi) mark in six blue characters written in a delicate but very mannered calligraphy, which seems to be peculiar to this type of ware, and to a few choice clair de lune and celadon vases of similar form and make."*

Fig 103.1 Kangxi Mark & Period (Reject) Peachblooms

	(a)	(b)
Type:	Beehive Brush Washer (Taibo Zun)	Beehive Brush Washer (Taibo Zun)
Design:	Peachbloom	Peachbloom
Dimensions:	125mm diam	127mm diam
Mark:	Kangxi (1662-1722)	Kangxi (1662-1722)
Dating:	Kangxi	Kangxi

Fig 103.2 Reverse View

Hobson's reference to 'white-glazed porcelain' is not strictly correct, for as this illustration shows, a blue-white glaze was also used. In fact, I have seen two halves of a perfectly fitting paste box, the two inners distinctly different, one white, one whitish blue.

Fig 103.3 Close-up of Dragon Roundel

Fig 103.4 Jade Lid Showing 64 Ways of Writing the "Long Life" Character

Liu concluded following a study of the National Palace Museum collection and others, that *"marks of this type were all written by the same person ... one style of mark is written using a lineation brush, a type of writing brush resembling a needle in shape, without a belly. ... There often tends to be a rats tail effect at the end of a stroke. ... At some point, he changed to the type of brush used for writing the small standard script, which produced a more full-bodied mellower style of calligraphy"*. Liu also identified eleven copper red (presumably including peach blooms), two bean green (celadon?), one 'sweet white', one sky blue, and two underglaze red, all with this mark.

Curiously, the underglaze dragon roundel was not consistently drawn, and may be found with either a 'short neck' *(Fig 103.3)* or with a 'long necked' version.

I have illustrated the jade lid to show the 64 different ways of writing the Chinese 'long life' character *(Fig 103.4)* so readers may appreciate the difficulty in translating Chinese to English.

The footrims were always finely levigated and white as *Fig 103.5 & 103.7* show, while the glaze on the underside of these two *(Fig 103.6 & 103.8)* shows consistent black/brown spotting.

These two close-ups of the mark *(Fig 103.6)* show the usual extremely fine, almost non-existent, Kangxi bubble, plus one feature of the calligrapher's work which will often reveal the fake; the left hand 'J' shaped stroke (of the Xi character) is written in two distinct strokes creating a dark spot where the strokes overlapped. For those readers interested, Liu also identifies peculiarities in the calligraphy which can identify the genuine from the copy.

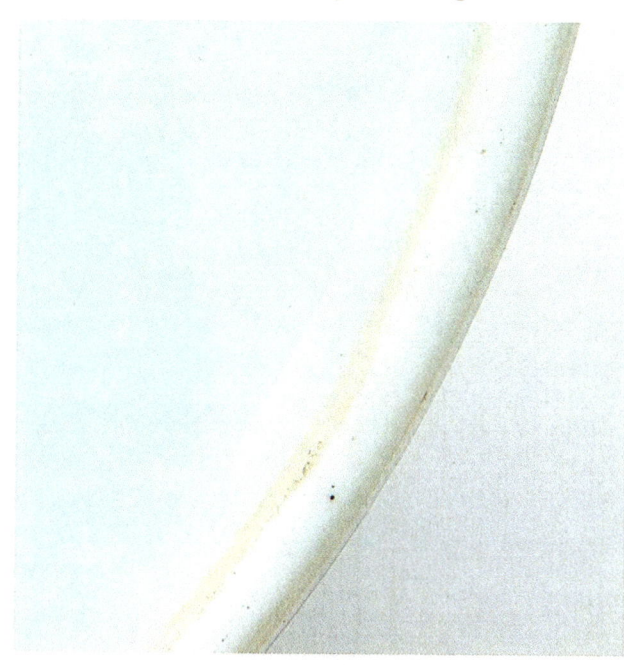

Fig 103.5 Footrim of Fig 103.1(a)

Interestingly, both of the exteriors of these two brush washers show signs of extensive use, another point to watch for. Also, although most of the fakes I have seen have duplicated this feature, the glaze runs out into an even white line around the footrim.

In 1996, I had the opportunity of handling the eight different shaped peach blooms, all allegedly genuine, auctioned by Christies in Hong Kong. On two occasions, for over an hour, I inspected and measured these pieces which Christies had marked as the Jinguantang collection; but which every experienced collector and dealer recognised, as they had appeared on the front cover of a museum publication, as coming from the Tsui Museum of Art. There was considerable disquiet at the preview in relation to this set of eight, and Christies did not help matters by having no one there who could answer queries about them. At the auction itself, Christies announced that one of the vases had had its whole base replaced, and one piece (the apple-shaped brush washer) was re-evaluated as a later copy.

In my opinion, which was shared by at least one other experienced Hong Kong dealer, one other piece (the Taibo Zun) was also not Kangxi mark and period, but a later copy.

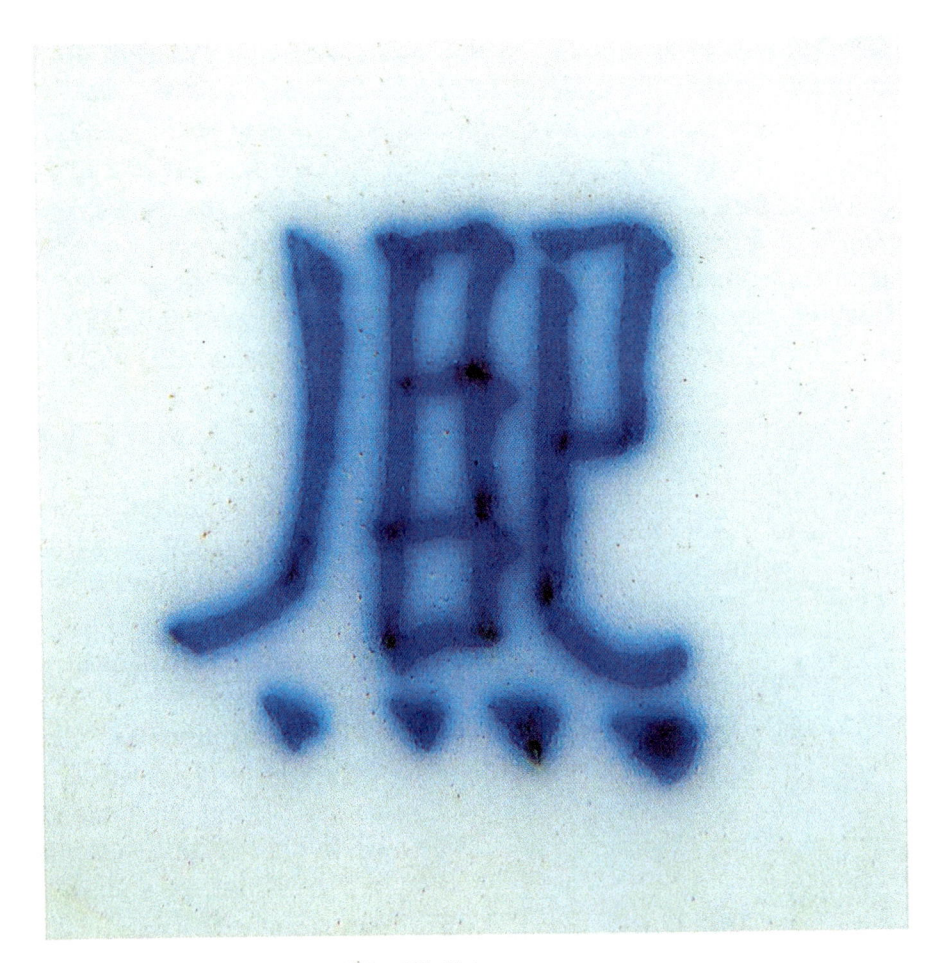

Fig 103.6 Close-up of Mark of Fig 103.1(a)

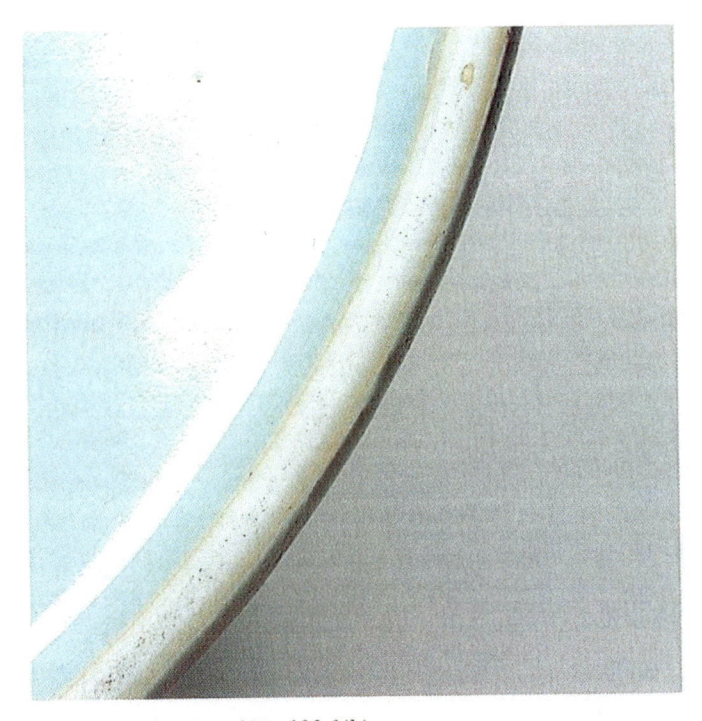

Fig 103.7 Footrim of Fig 103.1(b)

Fig 103.8 Close-up of Mark of Fig 103.1(b)

This collection was bought by the Baur Gallery in Geneva, who now baldly proclaim the set as genuine, in spite of Christies' disclaimer; let alone other experts' reservations. It would seem that the peach bloom glaze was only made for a short period in the Kangxi reign, possibly due to the advent of the famille rose enamels. But it did reappear again in Yongzheng and also Qianlong, but evidently not with porcelains of the eight Kangxi shapes.

It is interesting to observe the change in the red colour over these reigns, which readers may like to compare in Qian Zhenzong and Xue Gui Sheng's book (p 389).

Fig 104.1 Sacrificial Red, Qianlong Period (1736-1975)

Type: Saucer Dish
Design: Sacrificial Red
Dimensions: 180mm diam
Mark: Qianlong (1736-1795)
Dating: Qianlong

Fig 104.2 Reverse View

Readers will find numerous examples of Kangxi and Yongzheng red glazed porcelains illustrated in most of the major collection publications.

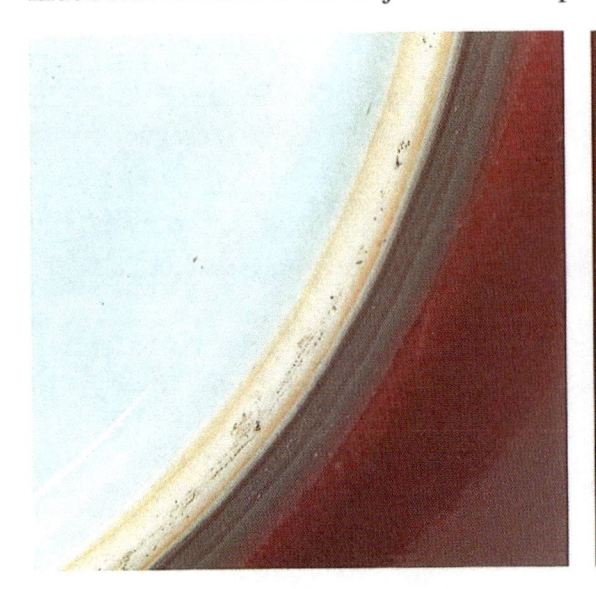

Fig 104.3 Footrim of Fig 104.1   *Fig 104.4 Glaze of Fig 104.1*

Fig 104.5 Qianlong Reign Mark of Fig 104.1

The sacrificial glaze *(Fig 104.1)* of this Qianlong mark and period saucer dish, is exceptionally dark, but note the Qianlong Imperial characteristics, a beautifully levigated iron yellow/orange footrim and the standardised beautifully written Qianlong reign mark.

Especially note how the glaze stops evenly at the footrim, a feature of almost all 18th Century red-glazed porcelains.

Bushell noted, circa 1895, commenting on a then modern 'sang-de-boeuf' vase:

> *"... the foot of the vase has had to be ground on the wheel to remove drops of glaze that have 'run' down during the firing. It is impossible to remove all traces of such drops, which usually occur in modern pieces of the kind - never on the old, when the glaze, which is uniformly distributed throughout, always terminates below in a straight line of mathematical regularity, and the foot of the vase exhibits no marks of the polishing wheel. The glaze in the new pieces is much more fluescent, so that the colour tends to run down, and the upper rim of the vase is often left perfectly white".*

Hobson, writing some 20 years later, commented:

> *"Even the best, however, of these wares should be recognised by inferiority of form and material, and in the case of red the fluescent glaze will be found in the modern pieces to have overrun the footrim, necessitating grinding of the base rim."*

I accept the fact that there is the odd exception to Bushell and Hobson's observations (notably some flambe glazes), but in the overwhelming majority of cases, they were correct. This should not encourage readers to believe that just because a piece has not been ground, it must be old; but if the excess glaze has been ground or chipped off the base, it may safely be concluded that the item was made after 1865.

Many Chinese dealers in particular, consistently misdate these ground vases to the 18th Century.

Fig 105.1 Qianlong Period Sacrificial Glazes

	(a)	(b)
Type:	Saucer Dish	Dish
Design:	Sacrificial Red	Sacrificial Red
Dimensions:	178mm diam	212mm diam
Mark:	Qianlong Kaishu Mark (1736-1795)	Qianlong Seal Mark (1736-1795)
Dating:	Qianlong	Qianlong
Courtesy:	Oliver Watson	Oliver Watson

The two dishes *(Fig 105.1)* are exceptions which break the rules. The smaller saucer dish *(Fig 105.1(a))* is marked with the rare six character kaishu script Qianlong mark, possibly indicating that it was made in the first two years of the reign, before the mark was standardised.

The neighbouring dish is of a colour which I believe the Chinese call donkey liver, but never having been to a donkey abattoir, I cannot be certain of this. Crackle glaze on 18th Century sacrificial red porcelains is not the norm, but as this piece shows, extensive crackling could occur.

Fig 105.2 Reverse View

Fig 105.3 Glaze of Fig 105.1(a)   *Fig 105.4 Glaze Bubble of Fig 105.1(a)*

The red glaze close-ups *(Fig 105.3 & 105.4)* show a fine bubble, in the latter case interspersed with crackle, while the mark close-ups show again the very fine bubbles (almost non-existent on one), which were a feature of many of the 18th Century wares.

So too are the orange/yellow footrims and distinctly blue glaze of the undersides, marred only by the odd defect in the glaze on the underside; like the glaze crawl seen on the bases of these pieces.

Fig 105.5 Glaze of Fig 105.1(b)

Fig 105.6 Qianlong Mark of Fig 105.1(b)

In my experience, the majority of Chinese dealers cannot tell the difference between a glaze and an enamel, so the pieces *(Fig 106.1)* provide the opportunity not only to clarify this point, but to distinguish between the 18th and late 19th Century red enamels.

The little sauce dish, in a pink/red enamel which the Chinese (translated) call 'lipstick pink', is Qianlong (1736-1795) mark and period. The saucer also bears a Qianlong mark, but the grey glaze, kiln adhesions, and greyish footrim indicate a date of manufacture, either late in the Tongzhi or early in the Guangxu eras (circa 1870-1880).

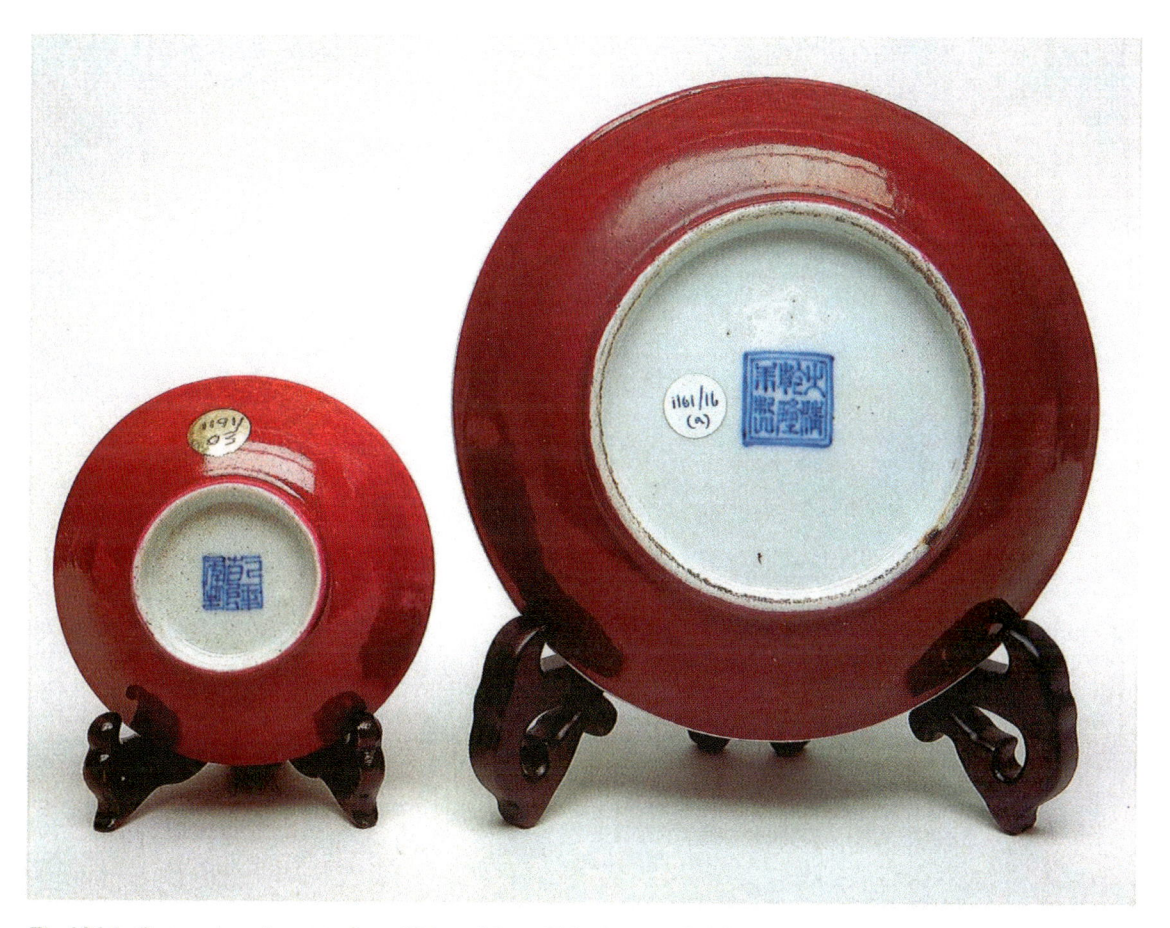

Fig 106.1 Comparison between Late 18th and Late 19th Century Red Enamels

	(a)	(b)
Type:	Sauce Dish	Saucer
Design:	Pink/Red Enamel	Red Enamel
Dimensions:	87mm diam	150mm diam
Mark:	Qianlong (1736-1795)	Qianlong (1736-1795)
Dating:	Qianlong	Circa 1870-1880

The Qianlong mark on the sauce dish *(Fig 106.2)* shows the fine 18th Century bubble and depth of glaze. Note also the debris spots, which are a definite indicator of age, and were illustrated previously on pieces which dated as early as Kangxi, or as late as the Republic. I assume this is a recurring problem with using a wood fired kiln, as I have never seen this feature on the modern fakes, fired in gas kilns.

The fake Qianlong mark *(Fig 106.3)* has the split lines (as distinct from hollow lines) which we have seen earlier on Guangxu marks. (See the third stroke down on the top left hand character.)

Fig 106.2 Qianlong Mark of Fig 106.1(a)

Fig 106.3 Qianlong Mark (Fake) of Fig 106.1(b) Circa 1870 - 1880

Fig 107.1 Late 18th and Early 19th Century Red Decoration

	(a)	(b)
Type:	Saucer	Plate
Design:	Underglaze red bats	Pink/Red Enamel
Dimensions:	160mm diam	188mm diam
Mark:	Qianlong (1736-1795)	Jiaqing (1796-1820)
Dating:	Qianlong	Jiaqing
Courtesy:	Oliver Watson	Oliver Watson

Fig 107.2 Reverse View

Underglaze red pieces which are mark and period of Qianlong are rare, and the bat decorated saucer *(Fig 107.1(a))* is only one of two that I can recall handling. Towards the end of the 18th Century, at least one private kiln mastered the technique of firing underglaze red; and they must have continued until the early Jiaqing years, for I have seen a number of pieces with one or other of these marks. Often they were left unmarked as those in *Fig 108.1* show.

The plate *(Fig 107.1(b))* has been covered in a red enamel, possibly, but not necessarily, after the Jiaqing potters lost the art of underglaze red firing. Readers should observe this greyish blue glaze and closely written mark for it is a frequently recurring feature of the Jiaqing period (1796-1820).

Fig 107.3 Underglaze Red of Fig 107.1(a)

Fig 107.4 Red Enamel of Fig 107.1(b)

The cloudy 'cracked ice' bubbles of the late Qianlong are seen above the underglaze red and blue *(Fig 107.3)*, while the close-up of the Jiaqing enamel *(Fig 107.4)*, shows the absence of bubbles which distinguish an enamel covering from a glaze; the glaze as we have seen, being bubbled.

Imperial underglaze red porcelains of the Jiaqing reign (1796-1820) are very rare, indicating that the person who knew the secret of firing (and jealously guarded it) had probably died. I have seen a number of 'minyao' Jiaqing mark and period red glazed saucers, but regrettably had none to illustrate at the time of photographing. Of course, another factory mass produced rather coarse underglazed red decorated dishes, an example of which was illustrated *Fig 27.1*, but there is some doubt that these came from Jingdezhen.

In the succeeding Daoguang reign (1820-1850), the underglaze red was again mastered, the glaze controlled *(Fig 109.3 & 109.4)* to end in an even line of the footrim edge. (It is believed that the potters applied a line of white glaze first, into which the red ran and stopped.)

Fig 108.1 Unmarked Red Glazed Saucers, Late 18th Century

Fig 108.2 Reverse View

Fig 109.1

	(a)	(b)
Type:	Saucer	Saucer Dish
Design:	Sacrificial Red	Sacrificial Red
Dimensions:	182mm diam	210mm diam
Mark:	Daoguang (1820-1850)	Daoguang (1820-1850)
Dating:	Daoguang	Daoguang

Fig 109.2 Reverse View

194

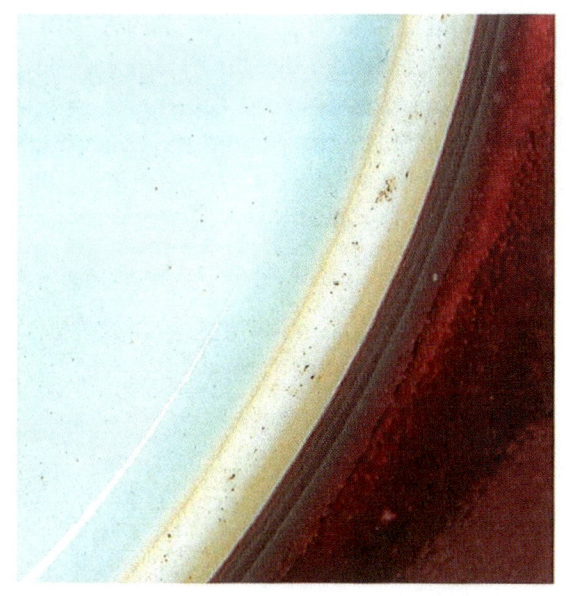

Fig 109.3 Footrim of Fig 109.1(a)   *Fig 109.4 Glaze of Fig 109.1(a)*

If the footrims of the two Daoguang mark and period red-glazed saucers *(Fig 109.3 & Fig 109.6)* are compared with the Qianlong examples earlier *(Fig 104.3)*, the orange colour is now missing, replaced by a white/yellow body with a yellow streak abutting the glaze.

Fig 109.5 Daoguang Mark of Fig 109.1(a)

Comparison of the two Imperial Daoguang reign marks *(Fig 109.5 & Fig 109.8)* shows they were not written by the same hand, but readers with Daoguang Imperial porcelains will be able to compare the calligraphy as there was probably no more than a few Imperial calligraphers in this reign. The mark on *Fig 35.3*, for example, is identical to that of *Fig 109.5*. The mark of *Fig 109.8* shows the beginnings of 'hollow line', one of the more useful dating tools for porcelains of the late 19th and early 20th Centuries.

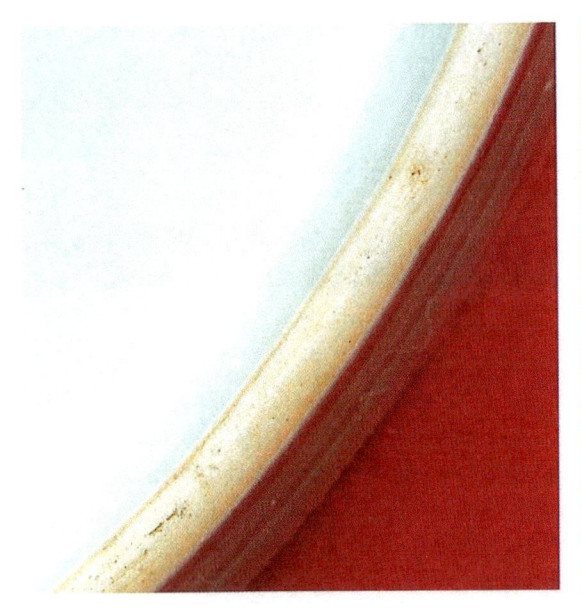

Fig 109.6 Footrim of Fig 109.1(b)

Fig 109.7 Glaze of Fig 109.1(b)

Fig 109.8 Daoguang Mark of Fig 109.1(b)

Fig 110.1 Red Glazes and Underglaze Red Decoration of the Daoguang Period (1820-1850)

	(a)	(b)	(c)
Type:	Miniature Vase	Brush Washer	Wine Cup
Design:	Sacrificial Red	Underglaze Red Phoenix	Sacrificial Red
Dimensions:	102mmH	127mm diam	66mm diam x 40mmH
Mark:	Xuande (1426-1435)	Chenghua	Nil
Dating:	Daoguang (1820-1850)	Daoguang (1820-1850)	Daoguang (1820-1850)

Fig 110.2 Reverse View

At least one private factory in the Daoguang period obtained mastery again of the underglaze red firing, largely concerning itself with the manufacture of small pieces, like the vases, brushwashers, wine cups and snuff bottles of *Fig 110 & 111*.

Fig 111.1 Underglaze Red Snuff Bottles

	(a)	(b)	(c)	(d)
Type:	Snuff Bottle	Snuff Bottle	Snuff Bottle	Snuff Bottle
Design:	Eagle	Rabbit	Fish	Camel
Dimensions:	84mmH	80mmH	84mmH	84mmH
Mark:	None	Fish	Fish	Qianlong (1736-1795)
Dating:	Daoguang (1820-1850)	Daoguang (1820-1850)	Daoguang (1820-1850)	Early Republic (Circa 1915)

The underglaze red of the Daoguang period (1820-1850) was a delicate colour, which tended, as the eagle and rabbit show, to fire a deeper colour in parts. In dating these pieces, it is important to look for the other Daoguang period features as well; a white body, often 'pin pricked' with little black spots, or a rounded footrim, or a yellow line where the glaze abuts the body. The camel snuff bottle *(Fig 111.1(d))* has a constant red colour, finely decorated blue, and most glaring of very late Qing and early Republic porcelains (in this case early Republic), a six character 'reversed S' Qianlong mark.

Readers of my earlier book must forgive me for republishing the Imperial Xianfeng mark and period (1850-1861) vase *(Fig 112.1)*. The new digital camera has enabled me to better show the features of this vase. Note especially the beautiful white body, with slight black pinholes, very blue tinged glaze, rounded footrim, 'countable bubble' glaze, and extremely fine calligraphy. Liu's translation of the Chinese historical records suggest that this vase can only have been made in 1853 or 1854, while the mark and known destruction of the Imperial kilns by the Taiping rebels provide a range between 1850 and 1855.

Fig 111.2 Reverse View

Fig 112.1 Xianfeng Imperial Yuhuchun Ping Vase

This vase must be one of the last sacrificial red glazed porcelains made in the Qing dynasty, for they were not to produce (perhaps with a rare exception), any underglaze red decorated pieces which would rival the earlier works.

As a consequence of the loss of the underglaze red technique, the Imperial requirement for red dragon or phoenix medallions had to be satisfied with overglaze magenta coloured enamels. Liu illustrates an underglaze red 'gall bladder vase' (p237), which he states to be Tongzhi ware (1861-1875) but I am uncertain if this may be just a mistranslation error, an error in dating, or just his opinion; because the same piece appears to have been dated by other Chinese authorities to the Kangxi reign.

When the Imperial factory was rebuilt, probably in 1866, the potters had lost the art of firing the sacrificial red glaze. Scherzer (see Tichane, p192) on his visit to Jingdezhen in 1882, recorded:

"Copper red, 'chi-hung', or sang-de-boeuf, so appreciated by private collectors, has not been made since the death of the last possessor of the secret of manufacturer. And for 20 years the factory administration has been making excuses to the throne for not being able to execute the command by her majesty to make 'chi-hung' glazes".

Fig 112.2 Reverse View

Scherzer also recalled: *"I also visited the lone, unique factory from which came the actual masterpieces, the vases with copper-red glazes called 'kung-houng'"*.

This factory was owned by a family named Ho, and Scherzer said of the Ho factory paste composition *"... this paste fires to porcelain at a temperature of around 1275-1300 degrees centigrade; it then has a pronounced grey colour ... and its transparency is practically nil ..."*.

He then added: *"The high percentage of iron in this porcelain causes it to lose its transparency and be closer to grey"*.

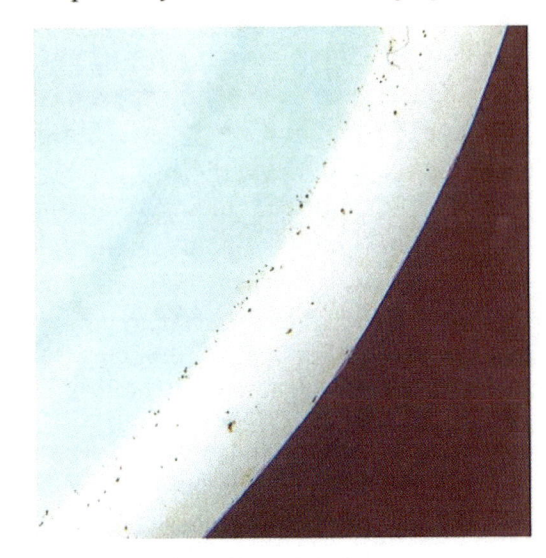

Fig 112.3 Footrim of Fig 112.1(a) 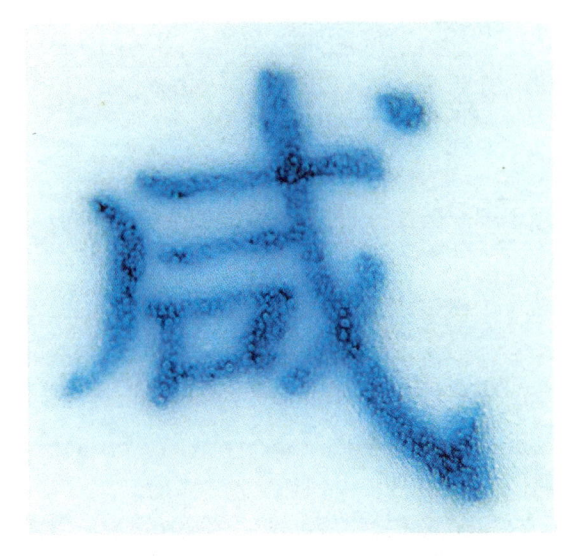   *Fig 112.4 Close-up of Xian Mark, Fig 112.1(a)*

Fig 113.1

	(a)	(b)	(c)
Type:	Elephant-Eared Vase	Lidded Jar	Marrow Vase
Design:	Sang-de-boeuf/Flambe	Sang-de-boeuf/Flambe	Flambe
Dimensions:	157mmH	270mmH	200mmH
Mark:	None	None	None
Dating:	Circa 1865-1890	Circa 1865-1890	Circa 1865-1890

It would be nice to say the three examples *(Fig 113.1)* are circa 1882, but I have been a bit more liberal and said circa 1865-1890.

Fig 113.2 Reverse View

Fig 114.1 Low Quality Sacrificial Red

	(a) & (c)	(b)
Type:	Wine Cups	Brush Washer
Design:	Sacrificial Red	Sacrificial Red
Dimensions:	48mm diam x 38mmH	120mm diam
Mark:	None	Erased
Dating:	Circa 1850?	Circa 1850?

Fig 114.2 Reverse View

Fig 115.1 Flambe Glazes of the Late 19th Century

Fig 115.1	(a)	(b)	(c)
Type:	Bowl	Censer (Brushpot?)	Censer
Design:	Flambe	Flambe	Flambe
Dimensions:	207mm diam	115mmH	235mm diam
Mark:	None	None	None
Dating:	Circa 1865-1890	Circa 1865-1890	Circa 1865-1890

I have stated the design on these three pieces *(Fig 115.1)* as 'flambe', but only the lip rims on the two censers show flambe, the rest of the body being covered in a 'treacle'-thick sang-de-boeuf glaze. Note the carelessly finished insides of these pieces, and the ground (or chipped) off overflowing glaze on the base.

Readers of my earlier book will recall seeing a somewhat similar orange base on a temple censer dated 1879 *(Fig 21)*.

Fig 115.2 Reverse View

Fig 116.1 Sang-de-boeuf Glazes, Late 19th Century

	(a)	(b)	(c)
Type:	Bottle Vase	Bottle Vase	Bottle Vase
Design:	Sang-de-boeuf	Sang-de-boeuf	Sang-de-boeuf
Dimensions:	190mmH	240mmH	150mmH
Mark:	None	None	None
Dating:	Fourth Quarter 19th Century	Fourth Quarter 19th Century	Fourth Quarter 19th Century

Fig 116.2 Reverse View

There is not much that I can add to these illustrations. The red glaze was extremely popular, and was applied to porcelains of practically all shapes and sizes. Note the grey bodies, as described by Scherzer, and the huge variety of finishes to the footrims and undersides.

Fig 117.1 More Red Glazes of the Late 19th Century

It is generally believed that the thick 'treacle-like' glazes date to the Tongzhi reign period (1861-1875), probably late in the reign, and it is interesting to find a Kangxi mark inside the little left hand 'guanyin' vase *(Fig 117.1)*, for if it is in fact of the Tongzhi period, it must be one of the earliest attempts at copying the peachbloom glaze. However, I personally have misgivings about such an early dating, for the celebrated American auction of the Morgan vase (for $US18,000) occurred in 1886; and two others to a Mrs Christian Holmes (for $US50,000) were even later. It seems likely that the attempts to duplicate these vases occurred in response to these huge prices.

The brown colour, reminiscent of the 18th Century 'Batavian' wares, seems to have been redeveloped in the Tongzhi reign and mastered in the subsequent Guangxu period. The absence of a mark on the brown glazed beehive shaped brush washer also suggests a date earlier than 1890.

Fig 117.2 Reverse View

The beautiful red glazed vase *(Fig 118.1)* was made by the Imperial factory, late in the Guangxu reign (1875-1908), and bears top quality incised Kaishu script marks to the underside. This vase shape is known to the Chinese as 'fanghu', and from the List of 1900, we know that 154 were made for the palace, and 1,474 for presentation; in that year alone. The white and black edges were a feature of both the Guangxu and Xuantong eras, as was the black (lacquer?) which adheres to the footrims *(Fig 118.2)*.

Even on the Imperial redwares of the late Qing, the glaze overran the footrim, necessitating a grinding off of the excess glaze.

The close-up on the glaze *(Fig 118.3)* shows a crackle feature of the Guangxu period, where the corners of some of the cracked sections break away, leaving small triangular shaped holes in the surface.

Fig 118.1 Imperial Fanghu Vase, Guangxu Period (1875-1908)

Type:	Vase (Fanghu)
Design:	Red
Dimensions:	300mmH
Mark:	Guangxu (1875-1908)
Dating:	Guangxu

Fig 118.2 Reverse View

Fig 118.3 Close-up of Glaze Fig 118.1(a)

Fig 119.1 Red Enamel Porcelains, Guangxu Mark & Period

Fig 119.1	(a)	(b)
Type:	Plate	Saucer
Design:	Red Enamel	Red Enamel
Dimensions:	247mm diam	135mm diam
Mark:	Guangxu (1875-1908)	Guangxu (1875-1908)
Dating:	Guangxu	Guangxu

The Imperial factory's inability to produce the sacrificial red, undoubtedly caused the change to a red enamel *(Fig 119.1)*. I have not shown the front of these redwares, as they have just the same red monochrome enamel. I have also seen Guangxu mark and period red bowls with plain white inners.

The close-ups of the 'Guang' character *(Fig 119.2 & 119.3)*, show a relatively thick finely bubbled glaze, over the expected inconsistently applied cobalt blue calligraphy.

The fanghu vase with tubular lugs was a popular shape in the Guangxu period, as was the variant with elephant-eared lugs *(Fig 120.1)*.

I wonder how many letters I will receive advising me that the flambe vase is 18th Century, undoubtedly the majority view of most Chinese dealers.

Fig 119.2 Close-up of Guang Character, Fig 119.1(a)

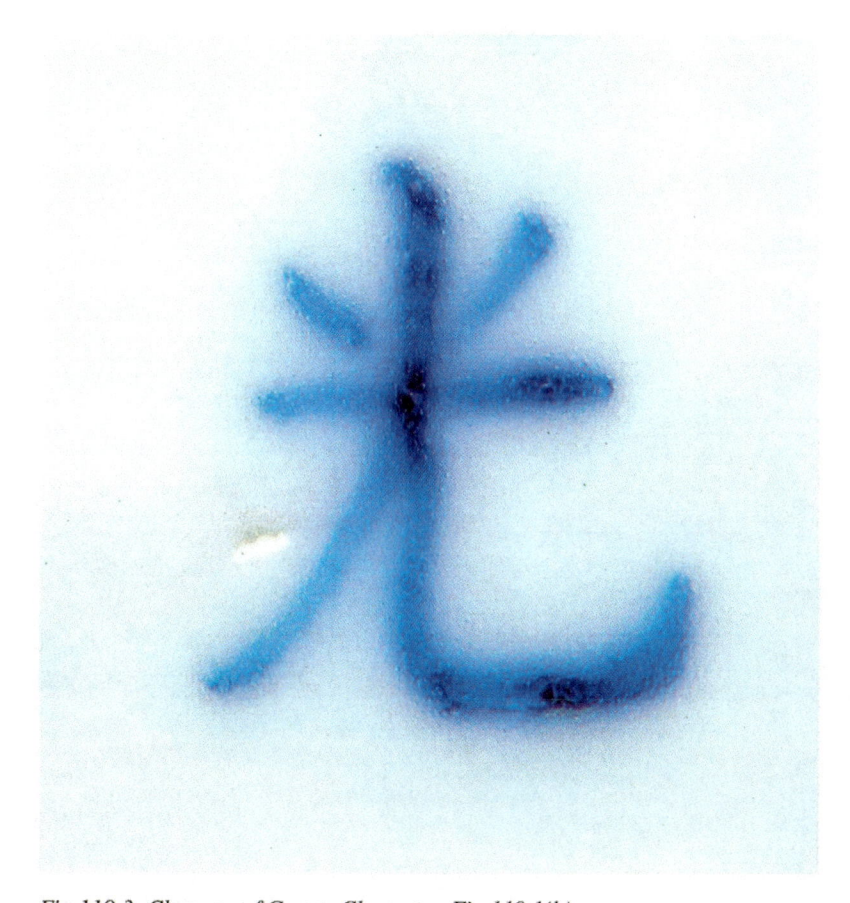

Fig 119.3 Close-up of Guang Character, Fig 119.1(b)

Fig 120.1 Fanghu Vases of the Fourth Quarter of the 19th Century (185mm-215mmH)

Fig 120.2 Reverse View

Fig 121.1 Red Glazed and Underglazed Red Porcelains of the Guangxu Period

As I approach the concluding part of this book, I regret that I was obliged, in the interests of cost, to combine a number of pieces into the one illustration *(Fig 121.1)*. There will be I am sure little agreement with my datings. Hobson recorded that the peachbloom glaze, was rediscovered in Japan at the end of the 19th Century and the potter was persuaded to transfer his secret to China; where, on the Chinese body, the imitations were completely successful. Admittedly, this was hearsay, but it seems probable that the peachbloom copies were not made in China until the early part of the 20th Century; probably in the last eight years of the Guangxu reign.

Fig 121.2 Reverse View

Many of these later porcelains will have a dirty grey/blue glaze and apocryphal Kangxi mark to the underside *(Fig 121.2)*.

I have yet to see an underglaze red porcelain piece bearing a period Guangxu reign mark *(Fig 118.1* excepted) an indication that while underglaze red may have been produced, it was not deemed to be of sufficient quality to be applied to the Imperial wares. The 'chimney-shaped' brush pot *(Fig 121.1(b))* must be in this category, and the fritting to the rim was a recurring problem in the Guangxu reign, probably as a result of using the Mt Kaoling kaolin.

Fig 122.1 Comparison of Guangxu (Fig 122.1(a)) and Modern Red Fakes of Kangxi Reds (Fig 122.1(b), (c), (d))

The brush washer *(Fig 122.1(a))* has almost the identical footrim to the Guangxu mark and period platter *(Fig 72.3)* and is a Guangxu period fake of the Kangxi red. The three other red pieces *(Fig 122.1(b)-(d))* are modern reproductions which have fooled even the experts.

Fig 122.2 Reverse View

Of the eight miniature porcelains illustrated *(Fig 123.1)*, only the little fish decorated bird feeder, in my opinion, dates to the Daoguang period (1820-1850), the very white footrim and delicate shade of red being the important identifying features. Initially, I believed that the two neighbouring red glazed snuff bottles were also early 19th Century, but I feel these are probably very late Qing, after 1900. The underglaze blue and red snuff bottle *(Fig 123.1(d))* has the badly misfired red, about which Scherzer in 1882 observed *"the dark, wine-red shade that it gives is rarely successful and again only on small pieces"*.

Fig 123.1 Underglaze Red and Red Glazes, Circa 1830-1930

I would speculate a similar circa 1880 date for the central bright red glazed snuff bottle, but these pieces can be difficult to date exactly, and a 20th Century dating is possible. The underglaze blue and red snuff bottle, third from right, has a similar pink colour to a lidded bowl in the Victoria & Albert Museum, which I discussed in my earlier book. Although the Guangxu reign mark appears on (from memory) the lid, and the bowl itself has underglaze red decoration, this is a 'matched' set and I reject a Guangxu dating. But it is possibly either Xuantong period (1909-1912) or more likely early Republic.

The two right hand underglaze red examples have apocryphal Yongzheng reign marks and were probably made circa 1915 to 1930.

Fig 123.2 Reverse View

Fig 124.1 'Peachbloom' Glazes 1900-1935

The traditional viewpoint has been to date 'peachblooms' of the type shown *(Fig 124.1)* to the late Qing, but if we accept Hobson's commentary, then they can only have been made after 1900 at the earliest. In my opinion, only the small guanyin vase is likely to be late Qing, as it has an apocryphal Ming Chenghua mark and late Guangxu-like fritting. Peachblooms of course were never made in the Ming dynasty, and all of the other pieces have Kangxi marks, the reign which they sought to emulate.

The 'peachbloom' fish saucer is an absolute rarity, for it is marked "Jingdezhen, 8th day of the 12th month 1934", giving us a clue to the date of manufacture of the other pieces. Note that the 'apple-shaped' brushpot in the centre of the group, has had its neck broken and turned down.

There is an extraordinary range of calligraphic styles, indicating a number of potters must have been responsible for writing the marks, and only the two front left and right pieces (the lidded box and conical brush pot) appear to have the marks written by the same hand.

Fig 124.2 Reverse View

The larger close-ups of the lidded paste boxes show clearly the range of bodies, glaze colours, and footrims which were used on these 'peachblooms'. An important dating feature of the 1930s to remember, a point I should have made earlier, are the very finely turned bodies on some of these small boxes, brushpots and vases. Readers may like to compare the footrim on the uppermost box *(Fig 124.3)* with the brushpot of *Fig 84.3(b)*. Also, the relative absence of imperfections on the glazed underside and very importantly, the 'non-Qing' underglaze blue colour.

So important do I consider this saucer *(Fig 125.1)*, as a guide to dating these peachblooms that I have shown it in close-up. Note the distinctly different hue of the underglaze blue, similar to the 1928 censer which I illustrated earlier *(Fig 83.2(b))*.

In the absence of any published data on these 20th Century porcelains, dating will remain a matter of opinion. However, the two remaining illustrations *(Fig 126.1 & 127.1)* may prove helpful to future generations of collectors, for the former I believe are of the Mao period (1949-1976) and the latter post-Mao 20th Century. The four snuff bottles and the rear plate were purchased new in 1997.

Fig 124.3 Circa 1930 Lidded Paste Boxes in Peachbloom Glaze

Fig 125.1　　Type:　　　　　Saucer
　　　　　　　Design:　　　　Underglaze Blue & Red Fish (Peachbloom)
　　　　　　　Dimensions:　　130mm diam
　　　　　　　Inscription:　　Jingdezhen, 8th day of the 12th month 1934
　　　　　　　Dating:　　　　1934

Fig 125.2 Reverse View

So ends my preliminary look at the dating of Chinese red wares of the Qing dynasty. There are numerous gaps, not just in the items that I had available to illustrate, but also in my own knowledge on the subject. But this is a start on a subject which few authors have had the courage to tackle.

I trust that readers and reviewers will accept that subsequent research will detect some errors in my dating. If I am alerted to these errors or can be shown examples with either dated inscriptions or provenance of acquisition, I will attempt to rectify these errors within my lifetime.

Fig 126.1 Mao Period Red Wares (1949-1976)

Fig 127.1 Post-Mao 20th Century Red Wares (1976-1997)

CHAPTER TWELVE
ADDENDUM

The preparation of this book has taken me three years since "Allen's Introduction to Later Chinese Porcelain" was published in 1996. Having accumulated the large range of items that I have illustrated, sorted them into some semblance of order, and then photographed the pieces, it was not surprising that I would be offered more pieces which assist with dating. So rather than try rearranging the whole book, I have done what Howard did before me (in his remarkable book on armorial porcelains), and published an addendum.

Fig 128.1 Dated Underglaze Blue Porcelains

	(a)	(b)
Type:	Censer	Tea Pot
Design:	Dragon	Landscape
Dimensions:	210mmH	155mmH
Mark:	Guangxu 20th Year 1894	1938 (or 1878)
Dating:	1894	1938

The censer figure *(Fig 128.1(a))*, dated 1894, shows a style of border decoration and unglazed body, which may assist in dating similarly decorated but unmarked pieces.

Unfortunately, the teapot has a 60 year cyclical date equivalent to 1818, 1878, or 1938, and the Hong Kong dealer that sold it to me was adamant that it was 1878. However, I believe he just said this to boost its price, because the body and the blue colour are not what I have seen in the Guangxu period. So I am sticking to my 1938 dating.

Fig 128.2 Reverse view

Fig 129.1 Guangxu Period (1875-1908) Underglaze Blue

220

The four pieces *(Fig 129.1)* are all Guangxu (1875-1908) mark and period, the larger plate 190mm in diameter. The glaze does not fully cover the body on either the saucer or left hand cup, leaving a series of small 'pinholes' in the glaze, just visible at mid position (12 o'clock) in the photograph of the saucer.

The Chinese dealer that sold me the table screen *(Fig 130.1)* assured me that it had a dated inscription upon it. It has not, but I have illustrated it anyway, for it dates circa 1925 to 1940.

Fig 130.1 Republic Period Table Screen

Finally the little porcelain kiln tester (85mm x 36mm) was given to me by the Jingdezhen Yi Bao Ceramic Co Ltd in Jingdezhen in April 1998. The manner of writing these Ming marks may assist collectors in the future.

Fig 131.1 Porcelain Tester Circa 1998

CHAPTER THIRTEEN
A VISIT TO JINGDEZHEN 1998

After several months of planning, necessary to coincide my diversion from Hong Kong to Jingdezhen with various auctions in England, I eventually received confirmation from Hong Kong that the internal flight was booked. My friend and genial Hong Kong dealer, Mr Leung Tai, proprietor of Hop Wah Antiques & Art Co in the basement of the Hyatt Hotel, had kindly offered to make the travel arrangements and to accompany me to Jingdezhen. His assistance was to prove invaluable, being fluent in English, Cantonese and Mandarin, plus of course, some 30 years experience dealing in antique Chinese porcelain.

The flight travel booklet shows only two flights per week from Guangzhou (Canton), but the airline changes the schedule and my return bookings must be amended. As the airline computer only accommodates bookings one month in advance, and we are travelling over the Easter Holiday and Canton Fair period, we don't know until the last few days whether we are booked; and Mr Tai has to get the tickets in Guangzhou, because it is too difficult in Hong Kong.

I fly into Hong Kong from London on 5 April 1998, and the following morning Mr Tai and I take the 1 1/2 hour train journey to Guangzhou. The taxi ride to the airport from the station takes 40 minutes, no problem for Mr Tai as Cantonese is his native language. Translating Chinese into English is exceptionally difficult, especially where colours or types of porcelain are involved, and even for Mr Tai it is a problem. Fortunately, he carries an ingenious little electronic translator which not only translates English into Chinese (and vice versa), but also speaks to us in a robotic tongue. We use this little machine frequently over the five days, especially when discussing the technical aspects of porcelain, or the content of our meals.

At Guangzhou Airport, I find that CA (from flight CA1392) stands not for China Airlines, whose modern planes I have seen at Hong Kong Airport, but Air China; and our plane is a droopy-winged British Aerospace 146, which in my country would not even be permitted to drop fertilizer, let alone carry passengers. Its underbelly is peppered with roughly riveted patches, the overhead lockers don't all seem to lock, and one engine runs rough for the 1 1/2 hour flight to Jingdezhen. Twenty-five passengers for the 78 seats and mine is the only white face. The engine noise rises and falls from the rough running engine, but as there are four engines I'm not too worried.

As we fly into Jingdezhen, I am captivated by the scenery, for these are the mountains of the Ming dynasty paintings, with tree-covered peaks and beautifully terraced gardens below. Everywhere on the flat is wet, for this is a flood plain, and there has obviously been heavy rain.

It is amazing that a developing country like China can maintain a large concreted airport like Jingdezhen's for only two flights per week, but Mr Tai notices there are actually six flights; two others coming from Shanghai and Beijing. When I inquire why they are not in the flight schedule, he tells me it is because they are not recommended for foreigners.

My purpose in coming to Jingdezhen is threefold. Firstly, I want to acquire some of the best quality reproductions of the Qing dynasty, those which when filtered through the Hong Kong and UK auction houses reach as much as £10,000; well beyond my budget for this book.

Secondly, to establish with the Jingdezhen experts the dating of several controversial pieces I own, including a number of Chinese redwares.

Thirdly, to amble among the scrap heaps of the Qing dynasty potters, to visit the museums, and to photograph if possible the making of the best quality reproductions.

We take the minibus for the 25 minute journey from the airport to our hotel. At 5RMB each ($US.50¢), I wonder how a driver and conductor can live off such low charges and run the bus with its five passengers. Our route takes us past lines of retail porcelain shops and we return the following day to look over the wares on offer.

Fig 132.1 The Retail Porcelain Shops of Jingdezhen

Fig 132.2 Mr Tai and the Author in Jingdezhen

Most are relatively coarsely decorated and we learn that many of these are actually seconds; rejected by buyers and placed by the manufacturers for sale in the street shops. The streets are bustling, bicycles compete with cars and trucks, the odd pedacycle and even rickshaws. This is Beijing as I remember it 15 years before, the driver incessantly blasting his horn, totally unnecessarily, even in the few streets where horns are prohibited.

We pass the Customs barriers, a relic of the 19th Century (and earlier), still manned, still collecting taxes (or duty as they call it), from people transporting commercial goods within the province.

Jingdezhen is a grey and dirty city as the photo taken from one of the museums shows *(Fig 132.3)*.

Fig 132.3 Jingdezhen

Fig 132.4 A Kiln Chimney Rises from the Paddy Fields

But immediately adjacent to the city centre, the concrete roads criss-cross the paddy fields, and occasionally, the tell-tale sign of a large brick chimney indicates the presence of yet another porcelain factory *(Fig 132.4)*. I did not actually see a wood kiln operating, for all of the factories that I visited used modern gas-fired kilns.

Our first visit after checking into the Joint Venture Hotel, on the Monday afternoon, is to the Jingdezhen Shing Long Porcelain Factory, where the proprietor, Mr Lee Fok Sing, kindly shows us his wares and permits me to take some photographs.

Fig 132.5 Porcelain Carving Copying the 19th Century

The artist shown *(Fig 132.5)* is copying exactly a copy of a 19th Century brush pot, which is often referred to in the West as an 'arrow' vase. Nothing in Chinese porcelain history appears to be sacrosanct, and we find not only the fake marked wares of the older artists, like Wang Bingrong, but also fakes of the contemporary, still living, masters as well. However, in another factory, I attempted to get a 19th Century Canton famille rose punchbowl made, but was told "No, this a Canton design".

At the Jingdezhen Jiaying Porcelainware Co Ltd, we met Mr Huang Yun Peng, who kindly showed us his company's large showroom and factory. I photographed *(Fig 132.6)* one of his girls working on a duplicate of the magnificent vase which I previously illustrated *(Fig 102.1)*. The working conditions, by Western standards, in all of these factories were appalling and in every case the light was so bad that I had to use the camera flash. The artists, usually young girls, cannot continue with this fine work indefinitely, such is the strain on their eyes *(Fig 132.6)*.

The following day, at the Jingdezhen Yi Bao Ceramic Company Ltd, I was able to purchase the pretty green teapot *(Fig 101.1(b))* with the scene of Westerners, copying the 18th Century works.

Fig 132.6 Enamel Decorating

I was impatient to see as many of the factories, museums, and kiln sites as I was able, but no amount of pleading could get us out of a two hour lunch and dinner on every day of our visit. Our driver, who volunteered his services free of charge, also owned, conveniently, a restaurant, to which we were taken on several occasions. I had told Mr Tai that I would pay for all of our travel expenses, and then find that we are expected to pay for the first meal; not just for the two people we have been negotiating with, but about seven other 'hangers-on' who also came. I need not have worried for the ten courses plus wine comes to only 210RMB ($US26). Our guests then want to return the compliment and I find I am in an impossible position because every meal time I am owed or owe a meal; and despite my protestations, I never once managed to avoid these twice daily two hour compulsory mealtimes.

Every evening in Jingdezhen we have appointments with someone, the first with an 'entrepreneur' with snuff bottles to sell. I tell him via Mr Tai that I can buy the same pieces that he wants $HK390 each for, in Cat Street in Hong Kong for $HK250. The vendor then admits his cost is $HK170 but rather than sell 10 at $HK200, and make the equivalent of 40 x 25 minute bus fares, in less than five minutes trading, he 'stone-walls' negotiations at $HK390. Mr Tai buys three pieces, out of sympathy I am sure for my unreasonableness.

Negotiations on price were extremely difficult, frustrating and time consuming. One shop would have a vase for 16,000 RMB and another, its 'twin' for 750.

On the following days, we were to see most aspects of the traditional Chinese porcelain production, now fired in modern gas kilns. We visited the old wood-fired dragon kiln, but it had not, despite many stories I heard to the contrary, been fired for a considerable period.

Fig 132.7 Decorating the Vases

Then at one factory, whose name I did not obtain, we found the giant vases being made, some as tall as 9 feet 6 inches. Caught in the flash *(Fig 132.7)* an artist decorates his vases in a dark mud floored factory. It is amazing that in such a primitive environment, vases of such beauty can be made so inexpensively. I had never seen these underglaze blue (and underglaze red) monster vases in the West, and immediately ordered enough to fill a container.

The factories had never sent (or seen for that matter) a container, but eventually I was able to get a container lot trucked to Shanghai and thence to New Zealand; arriving only four months after my order. To my amazement it arrived as ordered, beautifully packed, with no damage, but the costs after manufacture were fully double again the costs of production. When I suggested that the 'duty' of 3150RMB should be paid by the manufacturer, I was politely informed that the manufacturer liked cash, not taxes.

Negotiating the price and order caused the entire factory to come to a halt, everyone standing around and, if possible, contributing, otherwise absorbing, the conversation.

We were lucky to be there as a firing had been completed, and watched in amazement

Fig 132.8 Opening the Kiln

as the kiln doors were swung open, to reveal ten 6 foot high vases just fired *(Fig 132.8)*.

The workmanship of this factory is truly excellent, and I have seen smaller examples of their wares, 'yen yen' vases in particular, catalogued as 17th Century in both Hong Kong and London auctions.

It was reassuring to see that some at least of the Jingdezhen manufacturers are today recognising the quality of their products, and rather than affixing the apocryphal marks of the Ming and Qing Emperors, are signing and dating these masterpieces. The 43 large vases and lidded jars which I purchased, eight of which have since gone to London, are all artist-signed and dated.

An introduction to Mr Lei Rui Chun, deputy president of the Jingdezhen Museum, was to provide me with the opportunity to gain the answers to a number of questions as to dating, especially of the redwares. Mr Lei gave freely of his time and knowledge, and showed Mr Tai and me around a number of the museums. I stopped on several occasions by the roadworks, poring over kiln sherds which in some cases dated back to the Tang dynasty. A fascinating experience, which I would like to repeat before I am too old to suffer the privations of life in Jingdezhen.

The manufacturers were amazed that I was able to distinguish the fakes from the genuine, and on two occasions I was asked to explain, via Mr Tai, what was wrong with their porcelain fakes. On both occasions, they slipped a genuine (one Kangxi, one Guangxu) old porcelain piece in with their new reproductions, and on both occasions, I detected them. They seemed impressed.

One evening, Mr Lei visited our hotel with a wealthy collector from Shanghai, bringing four 20th Century pieces which the collector wanted verified. We in the West have not yet caught up with most of the top 20th Century artists, some still living, whose works in China can now command tens of thousands of dollars. There is a 'sheen' to the modern enamel which was not present before the 1960s, plus a usually 'greyed' foot, which to me gives away most of these modern copies. The Chinese look with 'different eyes' and we could not all agree whether two of these pieces were genuine. I was convinced that they were all new, but I am not certain that it was only the Chinese courtesy that stopped Mr Tai and Mr Lei from agreeing with me; for the Shanghai collector was already embarrassed with his errors.

The return flight to Jingdezhen was not uneventful and I arrived in Guangzhou, my trousers covered in tea, courtesy of my neighbouring passenger and a pilot who flew through thunderheads. This trip is not for the fainthearted, but despite the problems of travel, I hope to return. The majority of the Chinese people that we met treated us fairly and reasonably. At times, I was embarrassed by their openness, their generosity, and their lack of guile. I cannot say I enjoyed their food, everything 'macheted' into small hunks of meat, bone, scales and gristle; but for a few days, with my own supply of snacks, I will survive.

Without Mr Tai, I would have been lost, and I must now convince his delightful wife to again look after his shop while he comes to Jingdezhen with me for a return visit.

CHAPTER FOURTEEN
CONCLUSION

I have now read and re-read the draft of this book several times, finally reading it looking not for what is there, but for what is not there. There are some glaring omissions, for example, Yongzheng mark and period porcelains, or the Nonya wares (Straits Chinese porcelains). And my focus on 'Chinese taste' porcelains, rather than export wares has not been helpful to collectors of the latter, especially with the recent appearance of modern fakes of export porcelain.

In October 1998, I was fortunate to obtain at two separate New Zealand auctions, a number of additional pieces, which hopefully will add to the value of this text as a guide to dating.

Fig 133.1 Early 18th Century Export Tea Bowls and Saucers

The translucent enamels of the famille verte decorated tea bowl and saucer *(Fig 133.1(a))* suggest a date of manufacture at the end of the Kangxi reign, circa 1710 to 1720. Delicately potted tea bowls and saucers, but decorated in the then new famille rose enamels, were a feature of the subsequent Yongzheng reign, from 1723.

The brown ground tea bowl and saucer *(Fig 133.1(b))* were made for the Dutch market in large numbers, where the design is known by the French name as 'cafe-au-lait'; or to the English, more commonly as 'Batavian' wares. These pieces date to circa 1730 *(Fig 133.1(b)* and 1740 *(Fig 133.1(c))*, and again readers can see *(Fig 133.2 & 133.3)* how the enamel translucency changed to opacity, in a relatively short period. Some 'Batavian' wares have in place of enamelled panels, floral decoration in underglaze blue, and the majority of these will date a little earlier to the first quarter of the 18th Century. Note the distinct blue tinge to the glaze of *Fig 133.1(b)*, a feature of many of the export wares of the Yongzheng period.

Fig 133.2 Famille Verte Enamel   *Fig 133.3 Famille Rose Enamel*

Fig 134.1

	(a)	(b)	(c)
Type:	Plate (Armorial)	Plate	Plate
Design:	Chinese Imari	Floral	Tree in a Courtyard
Dimensions:	222mm diam	230mm diam	230mm diam
Mark:	None	None	None
Dating:	Circa 1710-1720	Circa 1730	Circa 1740

The Chinese Imari armorial plate *(Fig 134.1(a))* according to Howard, dates to around 1710, but in my view may be a little later; for the body has kiln adhesions which were not common in the Kangxi period. An almost identical plate is in the Rijksmuseum, and is thought to have been made for the van Gellicum family. The museum dating is 1710-1730.

The other two famille rose decorated plates *(Fig 134.1(b)&(c))* were common export items of the second quarter of the 18th Century, the heavier potting of the latter possibly suggesting even a third-quarter date of manufacture.

Fig 134.2 Reverse View

Fig 135.1 Porcelain Rarities of the Early 19th Century

	(a) & (b)	(c)
Type:	Sauce Dishes	Bowl
Design:	Doucai (Dovetailing Colours)	Magpies
Dimensions:	113mm diam	160mm diam
Mark:	Jiaqing (1796-1820)	Daoguang (1820-1850)
Dating:	Jiaqing	Daoguang

The sauce dishes and bowl *(Fig 135.1)* are relative rarities from the early 19th Century, the former being decorated in the doucai (dovetailing) enamels, while the latter is marked with a rare six character iron red Daoguang reign mark, in kaishu script. Porcelains of the period marked with Daoguang iron red six character reign marks in kaishu script, are extremely rare, and most pieces with such a mark are of recent manufacture.

Fig 136.1 Horse Decoration - Late 19th Century

	(a)	(b)
Type:	Stem Dish	Lidded Bowl
Design:	Horses	Horses
Dimensions:	210mm diam	110mm diam
Mark:	Tongzhi (1861-1875)	Pseudo Reign Mark
Dating:	Tongzhi	Fourth Quarter 19th Century

Fig 136.2 Reverse View

The 'horses' pattern *(Fig 136.1)* was popular from the late 18th Century, where it is often found on underglaze blue dishes; the horses with the most mischievous, almost lecherous, facial expressions. The hexagonal stem dish has a Tongzhi (1861-1875) reign mark, heavily potted as were many of the 'minyao' wares of this period.

The 'horses' bowl has a 'pseudo' reign mark, possibly a potters mark, or perhaps a copy of a Yongzheng 'lozenge-shaped' mark. The potting, gilding and body are almost undoubtedly Guangxu period, late 19th Century.

The large bowl *(Fig 137.1(a))* has an unusual decoration of overglaze blue enamel panels and five iron red bats. Porcelains such as these, of good quality, were 'custom-ordered', in this case probably for a wedding.

The tea bowls are decorated with enamels which are very similar to those on the Guangxu mark and period cup of *Fig 70.1(e)*.

Just prior to finishing the text, I was very fortunate to obtain four additional dated underglaze blue porcelains, the first a candle stick dated 16 November 1866 *(Fig 138.1(a))*. This is the earliest dated piece I have seen to date, made after the destruction of Jingdezhen by the Taiping rebels.

The bowl *(Fig 138.1(b))* is also interesting, for it has in addition to a Guangxu reign mark, a dated inscription to 1900. Note the firing fault in the rim, an unfortunate reducer of value, but further confirmation of a Guangxu period dating (at 5 o'clock on the front).

Fig 137.1 Bowls of the Guangxu Period (1875-1908)

Fig 137.1	(a)	(b)
Type:	Bowl	Tea Bowls
Design:	Bats	Floral Branches
Dimensions:	158mm diam	95mm diam
Mark:	Guangxu (1875-1908)	None
Dating:	Guangxu	Guangxu

Fig 138.1 Dated Porcelains of the Late 19th Century

	(a)	(b)
Type:	Candlestick	Bowl
Design:	Bird in a Tree	Floral
Dimensions:	117mmH	123mm diam
Mark:	Dated inscription 16 November 1866	Guangxu and Dated Inscription 1900
Dating:	Circa 1866	Circa 1900

Fig 138.2 Reverse View

Fig 138.3 Close-up of Guangxu Mark of Fig 138.1(b)

The absence of any orange line abutting the glaze of the candlestick would seem to indicate that at least some of the potters had already changed their source of kaolin by 1866; not as the Chinese historical records suggest, at the end of the Tongzhi reign.

Fig 139.1 Pair of Chicken Cups - Circa 1930

Type:	Wine Cups
Design:	Chicken
Dimensions:	83mm diam x 76mmH
Mark:	Qianlong
Dating:	Circa 1930

Fig 139.2 Qianlong Mark from Fig 139.1

The photograph of my recently acquired pair of chicken cups, will terminate this book on a provocative note, for cups of this quality are regularly sold as Qianlong mark and period; and if not Qianlong, as late Qing.

However, the overriding certainty of a circa 1930 dating is in my opinion conveyed by the combination of the following:

1. The purity of the enamels and glaze.
2. The colour of the underglaze blue, which is similar to that used on the fine Republic pieces of *Fig 84*.
3. The 'hollow' line of the underglaze blue.

These pieces were undoubtedly copied from a genuine Qianlong original, even down to the unusual mark; which readers will note, differs from the standardised Qianlong Imperial reign mark. Copies of these 'chicken cups' are still being made today (see *Fig 93(b)* in my earlier book), but on those that I have seen, the calligrapher has inscribed the standard Qianlong reign mark; not this variant.

Fig 139 was meant to have been the final photograph when I obtained a few other interesting pieces, which compelled yet another visit to the photographer.

Fig 140.1 Dated Chinese Porcelains

Type:	(a)	(b)
Design:	Vase	Lidded Pot
Dimensions:	330mmH	150mmH
Mark:	Dated Inscription to 1886	Dated Inscription to 1925
Dating:	1886	1925

The two pieces of *Fig 140.1* enable comparison of the common underglaze blue decoration of the late 19th Century, in this case 1886 for the vase, and the artificially tinged blue, common to many of the Republic period porcelains; in the case of the lidded pot, 1925.

Interested readers may wish to find the dates by comparing with the cyclical dating chart at the rear of the book.

Fig 140.2 Reverse View

Fig 140.3 Base and Footrims of Fig 140.1

On the vase, the year marks are the second and third to last characters at the bottom of the second row from the left. On the lidded pot, they are the first and second characters in the third row from the left. These are 60 year cyclical dates so without any reference to the Guangxu reign, the 1886 vase for example, could be misinterpreted as 1826 or 1946.

Fig 141.1 Republic Period Fake of Yongzheng   *Fig 141.2 View of Cavetto*

Fig 141.3 Footrim Base & Mark of Fig 141.1

The curious little dragon bowl of *Fig 141.1* would fool many an inexperienced collector or dealer, who may buy it as a genuine Yongzheng piece. Decorated in the two colours allegedly reserved for the Imperial third rank concubine, it is immediately recognisable as a fake, in my view made circa 1920 to 1930, for the following reasons:

(a) The dragon only has four claws, instead of five.
(b) The footrim is too rough, visible even in the photograph.
(c) The mark is poorly drawn. Compare the genuine Imperial marks of *Fig 143.4* & *Fig 144.2*, and this one has been carelessly written.
(d) It has the same blue tinged glaze as was seen on the dated lidded pot of *Fig 140.1(b)*.

Fig 142.1 Bowl Made for the Thai (Siam) Market

Type:	Bowl
Design:	Thai Figures
Dimensions:	178mm diam
Mark:	None
Dating:	Daoguang (1820-1850)

The Chinese potters have sometimes made specific designs for specific markets and the bowl of *Fig 142.1* is such an example. In the early 19th Century, there was a thriving market for porcelain, primarily but not exclusively bowls and stem dishes (tazzas), to what is now Thailand, formerly Siam. Until the recent economic downturn in Asia, bowls such as this were commanding very high prices in the auctions and antique shops of Singapore. Note the metal bands, a common addition to Thai market porcelains, almost undoubtedly added in Thailand. These Thai export pieces are often referred to as Bencharong wares.

Fig 142.2 View of Cavetto

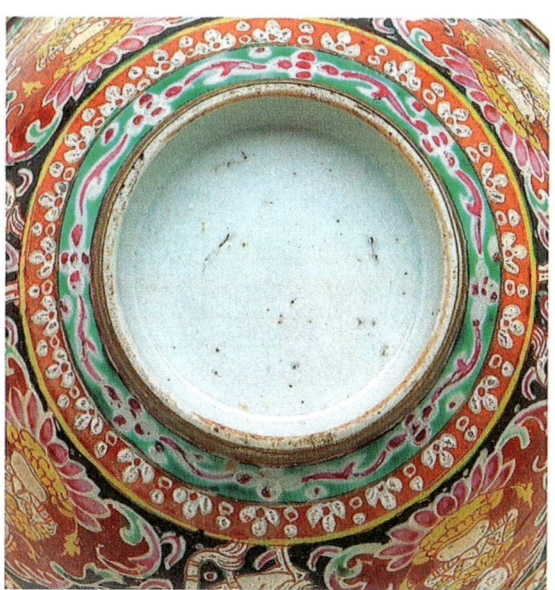

Fig 142.3 Footrim & Underside

Fig 142.4 Close-up of Enamel

I illustrated a similar dirty grey glaze in *Fig 2* of my earlier book, in that case on a bowl dated 1824. This glaze, coupled with the thick opaque enamels, often in strange unappealing colours (like the blue/green inner), will often date the piece to the Daoguang reign, between 1820 and 1850.

Compare the poor quality of this decoration with that of the Imperial saucer which follows *(Fig 143.1)*, and readers can see that not all 19th Century porcelain was of a low quality. Liu Liang-yu illustrates a similar saucer from the National Palace Museum collection in Taipei.

Fig 143.1 Saucer Made for the Guangxu Imperial Palace

Type:	Saucer
Design:	Bats & Peaches
Dimensions:	165mm diam
Mark:	Guangxu (1875-1908)
Dating:	Guangxu

Fig 143.2 Reverse View

Fig 143.3 Close-up of Enamels    *Fig 143.4 Close-up of Mark*

The accompanying illustrations of the rear view, mark and enamels highlight the general high quality of almost all Imperial wares. Pieces of this quality are now rare, and even though they are possibly not even 100 years old, still command very high prices. As both a dealer and collector, I have rather mixed emotions about selling such lovely items. In the case of the saucer, I was fortunate, because I bought a pair, sold one and retained the other, at least for the moment.

Fig 144.1 Very Rare White Imperial Bowl; Tongzhi Period

Type: Bowl
Design: None
Dimensions: 107mm diam
Mark: Tongzhi (1861-1875)
Dating: Tongzhi
Provenance: Weishaupt collection

Fig 144.2 Close-up of Footrim and Mark

I am at a loss to understand why many Chinese porcelain rarities, such as this wonderful white bowl, do not carry the premium for rarity, which would occur with say Worcester porcelain.

White glazed porcelain of the late Qing dynasty is extremely rare and I consider myself very fortunate to have been present when the dregs of the Weishaupt collection were sold in Christies South Kensington; without so much as a mention of their provenance.

To the Chinese, white is associated with death. In the Qing dynasty, white porcelain was made for the Imperial Temple of the Moon, and the List of 1900 records that both large and small white dishes, plates and saucer dishes were made in that year; but no bowls.

It is possible, of course, that it was intended to be enamelled. The footrim and colour of the mark are disarmingly similar to that of the Jiangxi Porcelain Industrial Co, illustrated earlier *(Fig 82.4)*; even though there are at least 35 years between them.

And there I must end this dissertation. Perhaps if I could summarise what in my view are the six most common indicators of a fake, as follows:

1. The absence of natural wear, or the presence of artificial dirtying or scratching (especially a grey footrim of uniform colour) which extends to unusual places (eg: the edge of the footrim glaze or undersides of bases or lids).
2. The excessive 'shininess' of the enamels and/or glaze (or unnatural dulling by whatever means).

3. The absence of imperfections in the glazed undersides (or insides of throats, lids, etc).
4. The absence of debris in iron red enamels or the absence of imperfections (pinholing etc) in other coloured enamels.
5. The absence of colour variations, debris, imperfections etc in the underglaze blue, and/or the appearance of 'icing sugar' bubbles.
6. The person offering it is an experienced dealer, and yet the price is too cheap.

I have not looked at the aspect of some of the most recent fakery, the copying of the works of the still living (or recently deceased) masters. Nor have I dwelt on the porcelains and stonewares made outside Jingdezhen, or their reproductions.

However, readers must remain alert for the new fakes, or the new innovations which correct the identifying features which I have outlined. Already, impurities are being deliberately introduced to the glazes and bodies, to simulate the natural impurities of the old wares. With time, the absence of other defects may also be remedied.

There are a number of dealers who will not thank me for this book; and auctioneers who will have to refund monies for misdescribed porcelains. Perhaps I might even succeed in getting a few museum pieces recatalogued.

And if I have restored some confidence to the fickle world of later Chinese porcelains, then hopefully there will be more collectors like myself who view fakes not as a problem, but rather as a challenge; and enjoy what has been for me a fantastic hobby.

It is both a time for caution and a time for opportunity, for I trust, now armed with this book, the majority of fakes may be identified; and the originals purchased with a certainty that was available previously, only to collectors and dealers of considerable experience.

I welcome correspondence from fellow enthusiasts:

A J (Tony) Allen
Allen's Enterprises Ltd
PO Box 33-194
Takapuna, Auckland
New Zealand
Ph/Fax: +64-9-479-3960
E-mail: Allen.Ent@xtra.co.nz

Table 1
PRINCIPAL REIGN MARKS OF THE MING DYNASTY
MING (明) 1368 – 1644

洪武年製	永樂年製 (a)	永樂 (archaic) (b)
Hongwu (Hung Wu) 1368 – 1398	**Yongle** (Yung Lo) 1403 – 1424	(b) is archaic script

大明宣德年製	大明成化年製	大明弘治年製
Xuande (Hsuan Te) 1426 – 1435	**Chenghua** (Ch'eng Hua) 1465 – 1487	**Hongzhi** (Hung Chih) 1488 – 1505

大明正德年製	大明嘉靖年製	大明隆慶年製
Zhengde (Cheng Te) 1506 – 1521	**Jiajing** (Chia Ching) 1522 – 1566	**Longqing** (Lung Ch'ing) 1567 – 1572

大明萬曆年製	大明天啟年製	崇禎年製
Wanli (Wan Li) 1573 – 1620	**Tianqi** (T'ien Ch'i) 1621 – 1627	**Chongzhen** (Ch'ung Cheng) 1628 – 1644

Table 2
REIGN MARKS OF THE QING (CH'ING) DYNASTY
QING (清) 1644 – 1912

Shunzhi (Shun Chih) 1644 – 1661	Kangxi (K'ang Hsi) 1662 – 1722	Yongzheng (Yung Cheng) 1723 – 1735	Qianlong (Ch'ien Lung) 1736 – 1795
Jiaqing (Chia Ch'ing) 1796 – 1820	Daoguang (Tao Kuang) 1820 – 1850	Xianfeng (Hsien Feng) 1850 – 1861	Tongzhi (T'ung Chih) 1861 – 1875
Guangxu (Kuang Hsu) 1875 – 1908			Xuantong (Hsuan Tung) 1909 – 1912

249

Table 3
A SELECTION OF 19th & 20th CENTURY MARKS FOUND ON CHINESE PORCELAIN

Shendetang zhi
(Made for the Hall for the Cultivation of Virtue)
Popularised by the Daoguang Emperor

'Dayazhai' Marks
(Associated with porcelain made for the Empress Dowager Cixi)
If genuine, late Qing, either Tongzhi or Guangxu Period

Jurentang zhi
(Made for the Hall Where One Dwells in Benevolence)
Hongxian Period circ 1916

Jiangxi Porcelain Industrial Co
1910 – 1934

'Hongxian' Marks
Allegedly made for the Hongxian Emperor (1916) but probably later

Shilu
(Stone Building)
Mark of Liang Duishi
Circa 1920 – 1937

Minguo
(Min Kuo)
Republic of China
1912 – 1949

Jingdezhen zhi
(Made at Jingdezhen)
Second Quarter 20th Century

'Jingdezhen' Mark Variants
Third & Fourth Quarters, 20th Century

IMPORTANT NOTE
Any mark can be reproduced. Never rely solely on the accuracy of a mark as a determinant of dating.

SELECTED BIBLIOGRAPHY

Anthony J. Allen
Allen's Introduction to Later Chinese Porcelain. 1996.

Art Gallery of New South Wales (Hepburn Myrtle)
Late Chinese Imperial Porcelain. 1980.

Art Gallery. The Chinese University of Hong Kong
Imperial Porcelain of Late Qing. 1983.

Gunhild Avitabile
Vom Schatz der Drachen (From The Dragon's Treasure). 1987.

John Ayers
Far Eastern Ceramics in the Victoria and Albert Museum. 1980.

C. and M. Beurdeley
A Connoisseur's Guide to Chinese Ceramics. 1974.

Michel Beurdeley and Guy Raindre
Qing Porcelain. Famille Verte, Famille Rose. 1987.

Anthony du Boulay
Christie's Pictorial History of Chinese Ceramics. 1984.

S.W. Bushell
Oriental Ceramic Art. 1896. Reprint 1981.

Chan Nam San and Mao Ngei-ing
Selected Pieces of Chinese Porcelain. 1979.

China Travel and Tourism Press
Life of the Emperors and Empresses in the Forbidden City.

Calvin Chou
The Hollow Line in Dating Chinese Porcelains. 1978.

Mark Chou
A Discourse on Hung Hsien Porcelain. 1978.

Christie's (Amsterdam)
The Vung Tau Cargo. 1992.
The Diana Cargo. 1995.

Christie's (Hong Kong)
The Jinguantang Collection. 1996.

Gerald Davison
The Handbook of Marks on Chinese Ceramics. 1994.

Dr. John Quentin Feller
The Canton Famille Rose Porcelains. 1982.

Gan Bo Cheong
Ming and Qing Porcelain Certification (Chinese text). 1993.

Wanda Garnsey and Rewi Alley
China. Ancient Kilns and Modern Ceramics. 1983.

Geoffrey A. Godden
Oriental Export Market Porcelain and its Influence on European Wares. 1979.

Elinor Gordon
Chinese Export Porcelain. An Historical Survey. 1977.
Collecting Chinese Export Porcelain. 1984.

Eleanor Hartstone
Rice Grain Porcelain. 1978.

Michael Hatcher (with Anthony Thorncroft).
The Nanking Cargo. 1987.

He Li
Chinese Ceramics. A New Comprehensive Survey. 1996.

Ho Wing Meng
Straits Chinese Porcelain. A Collector's Guide. 1983.

R.L. Hobson
Chinese Pottery and Porcelain. 1915. Dover reprint, 1976.

Hong Kong Chinese Snuff Bottle Society
One Thousand Snuff Bottles. 1993.

Hong Kong Museum of Art
Shiwan Pottery. 1988.
Brush and Clay. 1990.

David Sanctuary Howard
Chinese Armorial Porcelain. 1974.

David Howard and John Ayers
Masterpieces of Chinese Export Porcelain from the Mottahedeh Collection in the Virginia Museum. 1980
China for the West. 1978

Rose Kerr
Chinese Ceramics. Porcelain of the Qing Dynasty, 1644 to 1911. 1986.

Regina Krahl
Chinese Ceramics in the Topkapi Saray Museum. 1986.
Chinese Ceramics from the Meiyintang Collection. 1994.

Gordon Lang
The Powell-Cotton Collection of Chinese Ceramics. 1988.

Liu Liang-yu
Ch'ing Official and Popular Wares. Volume 5. 1991.

K.S. Lo
The Stonewares of Yixing. 1986.

Ma Xigwai
Blue and White Porcelain. Beauty of Ceramics. Volume 3. 1993.

S. Marchant and Son
Qing Mark and Period Monochrome Wares. 1981.
Nineteenth Century Mark and Period Porcelain. 1991.

Jean McClure Mudge
Chinese Export Porcelain in North America. 1986.
Chinese Export Porcelain for the American Trade, 1785 to 1835. 1962.

National Palace Museum, Taipei
Catalogue of the Special Exhibition...
    Yung-Cheng and Ch'ien-Lung Porcelain Ware. 1986.
Catalogue of the Special Exhibition...
    Ch'ing Dynasty Monochromes. 1989.
Chinese Ceramics, Ching Dynasty.

H.A. van Oort
Chinese Porcelain of the 19th and 20th Centuries. 1977.

Percival David Foundation of Chinese Art
Illustrated Catalogue of Ming and Qing Monochrome Wares. 1989.

William R. Sargent
The Copeland Collection. 1991.

Qian Zhenzong and Xue Gui Sheng
An Appreciation of Qing Dynasty Porcelain (Chinese text). 1995.

Herbert, Peter, and Nancy Schiffer
Chinese Export Porcelain. Standard Patterns and Forms, 1780 to 1880. 1975.
China for America. 1980.

Rosemary E. Scott
Elegant Form and Harmonious Decoration. 1992.

Sotheby's (Amsterdam)
The Weishaupt Collection of 19th and 20th Century Chinese Porcelain. 1995.

South East Asian Ceramics Society
Chinese Celadons and Other Related Wares in Southeast Asia. 1979.

South East Asian Ceramic Society, West Malaysia Chapter
Nonya Ware and Kitchen Qing. 1981.

Taoci
Jingdezhen Ceramics, 1949 to 1959. 1961.

Robert Tichane
Ching-Te-Chen. 1983.

Suzanne G. Valenstein
A Handbook of Chinese Ceramics. 1975.

S.J. Vainker
Chinese Pottery and Porcelain. From Prehistory to the Present. 1991.

Peter Wain
Heavenly Pieces. 1993.
The Kaynes-Klitz Collection. 1995.
Awaiting Spring. Qianjiang Art on Chinese Porcelain. 1998.

Wang Qingzheng
Underglaze Blue and Red. 1993.
Kangxi Porcelain Wares from the Shanghai Museum Collection. 1998.

C.A.S. Williams
Outlines of Chinese Symbolism and Art Motives. 1931 (Dover edition 1976).

Xiong Liao
Gems of the Official Kilns. Beauty of Ceramics, Volume 1. 1993.

Yang Yongshan and Yang Jingrong
Art of Folk Ceramics, Volume 2. 1993.

S.T. Yeo and Jean Martin (South East Asian Ceramic Society)
Chinese Blue and White Ceramics. 1978.

GLOSSARY
OF TECHNICAL TERMINOLOGY

alignment (or rotation) of the mark;
The majority of porcelains made at the Imperial factory for use by the Imperial household, were marked on the back with the reign name of the ruling Emperor. If the mark on the plate or dish is viewed from the back, then rotated through 180 degrees, the design should be exactly in alignment. Note that there are some exceptions to this rule.

anhua; (or secret decoration)
Incised decoration, applied to the porcelain body prior to glazing, and sometimes only visible when the piece is held to the light. This was a popular decoration, usually with five-clawed dragons, on monochrome Imperial wares.

Batavian wares;
Porcelains made in China for export to the Dutch and French markets, decorated with an outer brown (or café au lait) glaze, and traded through the trading post at Batavia.

biscuit decorated;
Enamel decoration applied directly to an unglazed but prefired porcelain body.

blanc de chine;
White glazed wares made at Dehua in Fujian province from the Ming dynasty and later.

bubble definition (as a guide to dating)
This refers to variations in the bubbles in the glaze over an underglaze blue stroke, visible when using a 15 power eyeglass, especially above the strokes of characters in a reign mark. The late 17th and early 18th century bubbles are usually very fine. Those of the late 18th and early 19th century, are often not well defined, are under a thicker glaze, having the appearance of cracked or crushed ice; while those of the late 19th and early 20th century, are often well defined and 'countable'. The bubbles on many modern (20th century) reproductions, by comparison, are like icing sugar; ie poorly defined.

buckling; (or warping)
A feature of many porcelains fired in wood kilns, and seldom seen on reproductions fired in modern gas kilns. It is often a useful indicator of some age.

burial wares;
Porcelain and pottery made to accompany the deceased in the afterlife.

clare de lune
A pale blue glaze, inspired by the jun wares of the Song dynasty. Popularised in the early 18th century, where it appears on Imperial porcelains of both the Kangxi and Yongzheng reigns, clare de lune was again copied in the Republic period.

café au lait;
See Batavian wares.

Canton famille rose;
Porcelain made at Jingdezhen from the early 19th century, but enamel decorated to order at the trading port of Canton (Guangzhou). The designs frequently cover much of the pieces, and include either panels of figures, butterflies, flowers and shrubs.

Canton pattern;
An underglaze blue variation of the willow pattern design, made for export (largely to America) from the early 19th century, which has no figures on the bridge. If there are figures on the bridge, the pattern is known as Nanking (Nankin).

celadon;
A high-fired green glaze which was the predominant colour until the 13th century, and the principal product of the Longquan kilns in Zhejiang province.

chicken skin;
A white enamel decoration of raised lumps, giving the appearance of chicken skin or goose bumps.

clobbering;
A term given to porcelains which have been overdecorated, or embellished, after manufacture, usually outside China.

concubines;
The Emperor, according to the Palace regulations, was entitled to a harem comprising set numbers of concubines of varying ranks; and each rank in turn was entitled to set numbers and designs of porcelain for their own use.

dated porcelain;
Porcelain which bears an inscription dating it to a specific year, sometimes to the month and day. If the date is in underglaze blue, the date was often contemporary with the potting, and provides a year of manufacture. Enamelled inscriptions were often added long after the date of potting.

Dayazhai;
A name given to porcelain which was popularised by the Empress Dowager Cixi in the late 19th century, bearing the Dayazhai mark, meaning Abode Of Grand Culture. The designs include a number of colour variants, but most have a magpie in a branch.

doucai;
Variously known as dovetailing, contending, joined or contrasting colours, doucai is a style of decoration which combines underglaze blue with overglaze enamels.

dragon;
The dragon was the symbol of the Emperor. In the Qing dynasty the Imperial dragon almost invariably had five claws to each foot, never four, and rarely three.

egg & spinach decoration;
A name given to splash glazed enamels, applied directly to an unglazed body, in green and yellow; sometimes with aubergine (purple) and blue.

eggshell porcelain;
Porcelain of eggshell thinness, perhaps 1 to 1.5 millimetres thick.

eight;
An auspicious number in Chinese mythology, giving rise to such designs as eight trigrams, eight immortals, eight Buddhist symbols etc.

enamel or glaze crawl;
A term used to describe an apparent shrinking of the enamel or glaze, where it pulls back and does not fully cover what was intended.

fahua;
A decorative technique which originated in the Yuan dynasty, where the motifs are outlined with strips of clay to form compartments for the different coloured glazes.

famille rose;
The name given to the 'foreign colours', of pink and white, first introduced to China circa 1710AD.

famille verte;
The traditional Chinese palette, prior to the introduction of famille rose, which was based on a translucent green enamel, complemented with enamels of yellow, blue, aubergine, turquoise and iron (rust) red.

flambé;
A reddish glaze which transmuted to an iridescent purple, blue and white, giving the appearance of flames.

guanguyao;
This is the Chinese name given to the confusingly named official old wares. They are commissioned pieces of generally good quality, made to order by the wealthy aristocracy, sometimes at the Imperial kilns.

guanyao;
Sometimes referred to as guan wares, this is the Chinese name given to porcelain made at the Imperial (Official) kilns for the Imperial household.

'hollow line';
A term coined by Calvin Chou to describe a recurring feature of many late Qing and early Republic underglaze blue decorated porcelains, where the particles of cobalt separated to the edges of the stroke; thus giving the appearance of hollow lines or railway tracks.

kaolin;
China clay, an essential component which, when combined with petuntse, formed the primary ingredients for making porcelain.

kaishu;
The standard written Chinese script.

'kitchen Ming' (or Qing)
A name applied to minyao porcelain made for Chinese domestic use.

Kraak porcelain;
An underglaze blue decorated porcelain, made for export to the Dutch markets in the late Ming dynasty, usually comprising segmented panels of decoration.

Levigation;
The smoothness of the paste (biscuit) established either visually or by touch of the unglazed parts, usually the footrim.

List Of 1900;
The official porcelain production list for the Imperial kilns in 1900, found in the palace archives.

Mandarin pattern;
An export design picturing mandarins, popularised in the late 18th century, usually to be identified by a mauve/purple enamel.

Minguo;
Chinese name for the Republic of China (1912 to 1949).

minyao;
The Chinese name for 'people's ware'; porcelain made for domestic (or export) use, as distinct from guanyao or Imperial wares.

nonya wares;
Or Straits Chinese porcelain. 19th and early 20th century Chinese export wares, made for the Singapore and Straits Chinese settlements.

orange peel glaze;
A name given to an undulating white glaze which has been applied unevenly, and usually overthickly.

peachbloom;
Derived from copper-oxide, and fired in a reducing atmosphere, peachbloom is a pinkish/red glaze which frequently has flushes of green or black. In the Kangxi period, only eight different shapes were made in the Imperial kilns

phoenix;
As the dragon was the symbol of the Emperor, so the phoenix was the emblem of the Empress. Consequently the phoenix is often seen in conjunction with the dragon.

pinholing;
Small holes which appear in the body of some porcelains of the Daoguang and Xianfeng periods. Not to be confused with potato or palm eyes, which are small black flecks in the glaze, and can occur virtually in any period.

'reversed S';
A method of writing the Qianlong reign mark in Seal Script, where the S-shaped part of the character Qian is reversed. This mark is often found on copies made in the Republic period.

ricegrain;
A type of decoration where a pattern of small rice grain size holes are cut through the body prior to glazing. The translucent glaze covers the holes after firing. Ricegrain decoration does not appear to have been used before the 18th century.

ridge in the roundedness (loach back);
A ridge in the roundedness of the footrim, often found on the late Qing Imperial yellow, and yellow, green and aubergine saucers.

rose medallion;
An export design which seems to have developed after circa 1850, where the traditional Canton famille rose panels of birds, flowers and or figural scenes, is complemented by a round gilded medallion.

ruby back;
The ruby backed enamel of plates & dishes was purportedly reserved for the Emperor's birthday.

saggar (or seggar);
A ceramic refractory box, used to protect porcelain from the direct heat of the flame during firing. The saggar usually held between one and ten pieces.

sang de boeuf;
A vivid red glaze, sometimes known as oxblood.

sgraffito decoration;
Sometimes known as graviata, sgraffito generally refers to an enamel ground which has been delicately incised with stylised patterns of floral or feather-like scrolls.

Shiwan stonewares;
Glazed ceramics, including sculptural figures, made at Foshan in Guangdong province, usually covered with a red, flambé or jun blue glaze.

'split lines';
A feature of some late Qing and early Republic underglaze blue decorated porcelains, where the strokes of the blue appear to have split; sometimes giving the appearance of crazed (burnt) paint.

stapling;
A method of repairing broken porcelain, by fixing with metal staples, probably not much used after circa 1950 when better glues became available.

teadust glaze;
An olive or yellowish green glazed, often speckled, which was reputedly reserved for the Emperor's use. There are numerous examples to refute this assertion.

wax seals;
Seals applied by Chinese government antique inspectors to certify that the porcelain to which it was applied, were approved for export. It is no guarantee of age. In some parts of China, the wax seal has been superseded by a red paper label.

yellow;
In Imperial porcelain, a monochrome colour reserved for the Emperor, Empress, and Empress Dowager.

Yixing stonewares:
A range of red, brown, green and purple stonewares, particularly teawares, made at Yixing, Jiangsu province.

zhuanshu;
The Chinese name for seal script, commonly used as an alternative to kaishu script for writing reign marks on the undersides of porcelain.

INDEX

acid treatment (simulating age/wear); 25
alignment of mark; 22, 73
American market; 178, 205
anhua (secret) decoration; 104, 136
antimony; 57, 106, 158
armorial porcelain; 16, 232
arrow vases; 83, 84, 226
Art of Folk Ceramics; 12
ashes (ink) box; 48
aubergine; 20, 21, 78, 107
Auckland War Memorial Museum; 170

bat decoration; 25, 99, 132, 191, 235, 236, 244
Batavian wares; 205, 231
Baur Gallery; 183
Bencharong; 242
birthday services; 108
biscuit decorated; 123
black flecks in glaze; 9, 17, 41, 144, 156, 189
black, marks; 9, 104, 105
blue, enamel; 164
blue, glaze; 38
blue, tinge, to glaze; 28, 38, 44, 231
Boxer Rebellion; 84
brown rim; 44
brush pot; 71, 82, 145, 178, 179, 203, 210
brush washer; 145, 157, 197
bubbles; 13, 15, 20, 26, 29, 33, 45, 55, 62, 75, 81, 92, 94, 95, 97, 120, 132, 134, 140, 144, 187
buckling; (see warping)
Buddhist emblems; 59, 60, 119
burial wares; 9, 48
Bushell; 72, 73, 128, 177, 185
butterfly decoration; 27, 101

café au lait; 231
calligraphy, quality of; 57, 73, 104, 136, 145
candlestick; 236
Canton famille rose; 113, 226
carved porcelain; 64
celadon, glaze; 40, 65, 129, 170, 178
censer; 23, 49, 75, 98, 203, 219
Chenghua, reign mark; 14, 197, 214
Chia Ch'ing; (see Jiaqing)
chicken cup; 237
Ch'ien Lung; (see Qianlong)
China, made in, mark; 101, 102, 114, 169
China, mark; 64, 112, 114

Chinese Government, Approval for Export Seal; 97
Chinese Imari; 24, 232
Ch'ing; (see Qing)
Ching te chen; (see Jingdezhen)
chopstick drainer; 75
Chou, Mark; 151
Christie's; 11, 24, 46, 181
clare de lune; 103, 178
'clobbered' wares; 35
cobalt blue; 129, 140
Concepcion; 14
concubines; 20, 78, 105
cong, vase; 131
copy; (see fakes)
cracked/crushed ice, bubbles; 31, 45, 192
cricket cage; 82, 83
custom-made blanks; 120, 154

Daoguang, reign; 40
Daoguang, reign mark; 39, 57, 61, 63, 195, 196
Daoguang, reign mark (fake); 61
dated porcelain; 67, 75, 110, 142, 144, 149, 151, 154, 160, 163, 164, 165, 167, 172, 214, 219, 235, 239
dated porcelain (fake); 18
Davison, Gerald; 64
dirt, applied simulating age; 9, 25, 94, 140, 172
diamond-shaped mark; 25
Diana (wreck of); 46
domestic ware; (see minyao)
double happiness; 12
doucai (dovetailing colours); 25, 26, 118, 142, 233
dragon, five-clawed; 58, 89, 98, 124, 144, 146
dragon, four-clawed; 75, 98
dragon scales; 98, 99

earthenwares; 10
Ebelman and Salvetat; 53
egg and spinach decoration; 124
egg shell porcelain; 164, 172
Emperor; 56, 136
Empress; 56, 136
Empress Dowager; 56, 136
export wares; 16, 27, 34, 37, 46, 50, 101, 231, 232
export wares (fake); 51

261

fakes; 5, 9, 12, 25, 87, 92, 93, 94, 101, 105, 106, 107, 131, 132, 146, 161, 173, 211
famille rose; 22, 25
famille verte; 22, 137, 231
Fanghu vase; 103, 206
flambe; 177-217
flaws; (see imperfections)
footrims; 43, 47, 128
fritting; 44, 65, 142

Garnsey and Alley; 148
Geng Baochang; 178
gilding; 38, 39
ginger jars; 53, 64, 122
glaze crawl; 187
glazed footrims; 164
graviata; (see sgraffito)
green and aubergine (purple) dragons; 20, 21, 78, 107
grinding of glaze overruns; 185
grooved foot; 24
Guangxi province; 12
Guangxu, reign; 89-134
Guangxu, reign mark; 91
Guangxu, reign mark (fake); 18, 88, 96
guanyao; 89
guanguyao; 89, 90

hat stands; 83, 84
hawthorn design; 53, 91
He Xuren; 162
Ho Factory; 200
Hobson; 22, 178, 185
hollow line; 26, 29, 61, 92, 142, 196
Hongxian, reign mark; 151, 154
horse decoration; 234
Howard, D.S.; 231
Hsien Feng; (see Xianfeng)
Hsuan Tung; (see Xuantong)
hu, vase; 103
Hunan province; 148

Imari; (see Chinese Imari), 24
imperfections; 20, 28, 83
Imperial; 29, 43, 51, 56, 73, 87, 89, 90, 103, 105, 106, 135, 186, 192, 206, 244
Imperial Factory; 25, 105
incense burner (censer); 24
ink (ashes) box; 48
ink stone (fake); 19
inscriptions; 79, 84
Islamic (Persian) inscription; 48

Japanese; 24, 69, 70, 123, 148
Jardiniere; 155
Jiangxi Jing Cheng Art Studio; 167
Jiangxi Porcelain Industrial Co; 141, 142, 155, 246
Jiaqing, reign; 43-51
Jiaqing, reign mark; 31, 45
Jiaqing, reign mark (fake); 50
Jingdezhen; 70, 73, 79, 123, 142, 147, 148, 176, 214, 223-230
Jingdezhen Jiaying Porcelainware Co; 175, 226
Jingdezhen Shing Long Porcelain Factory; 226
Jingdezhen Yi Bao Ceramic Co; 222, 226
Jiu Jiang Da Shing Company; 157
Jurentang, mark; 151, 152, 159

Kang H'si; (see Kangxi)
Kangxi reign; 13-24
Kangxi reign marks; 5
Kangxi reign marks (fake); 5
kaolin; 28, 43, 53
kilns, gas-fired; 226
kitchen Ming; 10
Kuang Hsu; (see Guangxu)
Kwan, Simon; 145, 148, 159

lamped vase; 159
lavender glaze; 132, 157
levigation; 15, 22, 26, 31, 71, 75, 78, 142, 185
lidded boxes; 48
Lim Suan Poh; 148
lipstick pink; 189
List of 1900; 107, 206, 246
Liu, Liang-yu; 28, 43, 53, 89, 181, 199, 243
Liu, Xiren; 159
loach back; (see ridge in the roundedness)
Longchuan China; 169
long life character; 180

magpie decoration; 132, 233
Mandarin pattern; 37
'Mao' period; 167-170, 217
mark and period; 178
marks, family (owner's); 58
marks, reign; 78
milky glaze; 10, 11
millefiore; 115
Ming dynasty; 9
minature vases; 17, 18
minyao; 31, 44, 79, 112, 170, 235
mortar; 67
Mt Kaoling, kaolin; 28, 43
Mudge; 116

262

Nanking (Nankin) pattern; 51, 101
Nonya wares (Straits Chinese Porcelain); 24

official ware; (see guanyao)
official old ware; (see guanguyao)
Om character; 46, 47
orange, footrim; 17, 28, 34, 41, 47, 63, 67, 71, 237
orange peel, glaze; 53, 110
oxblood; 177

palace bowls; 60, 61
Park, Mrs Barbara; 106
Peabody Museum; 116
peachbloom; 177-217
Pekinese dog; 46, 124
pendant borders; 164
Persian market; 49
phoenix; 112, 145, 146, 197, 199
Ping Shang Porcelain Co; 148, 151
plaques (panels); 110, 111, 148, 161, 162, 164
Puyi; 135, 151

Qianjiang, enamels; 84, 137, 156
Qianlong, period; 29-41
Qianlong, reign mark; 29, 30, 31, 33, 36, 39, 41, 185, 188, 190
Qianlong, reign mark (fake); 131, 169, 175, 190, 238
Qian Zhenzong and Xue Gui Sheng; 25, 50, 183

red, enamel; 191, 192, 208
red, glaze; 177-217
red, sacrificial (liver); 177, 183, 186, 194, 199
red, underglaze; 47, 177-217
relief carving; 64
Republic period; 33, 53, 141-166
reticulated, porcelain; 35
'reversed S', Qianlong reign mark; 33, 36, 128, 131, 145, 198
reverse decorated; 89
rice grain, decoration; 98
ridge in the roundedness (loach back); 20, 78
Rijksmuseum; 232
rooster; 122
rose medallion; 113
rotation, of reign marks; 22, 73

sand, adhesions; 113, 115
sandblasting (simulating age/wear); 25
sang de boeuf (oxblood); 6, 177
Satsuma; 69, 123
sauce dishes; 32
Scherzer; 20, 199

seconds, of Imperial wares; 29
secret decoration; (see anhua)
sgraffito, decoration; 45, 115, 157, 175
Shendetang, mark; 6
sherds; 100, 136, 142
shine, glaze/enamels; 27
Shunzhi period; 13
snow painting; 161
snuff bottles; 43, 57, 58, 127, 171, 198, 212
soap dish; 82
'soft paste', porcelain; 34
Sotheby's; 43, 61
spittoon; 101
split lines; 95, 100, 142, 189
spoons; 36, 49, 117
spur marks; 117
stapling; 14
stonewares; 10
starburst pattern; 46
Straits Chinese Porcelain; (see Nonya wares)
straw colour footrim; (see also orange and yellow) 29, 38

table screens; 163, 221
Taiping, rebellion; 72, 79, 198, 235
Tao Kuang; (see Daoguang)
tea dust glaze; 103
tea caddies; 71
tea services; 108
temples; 136, 246
Thai market; 242
tiles; (see plaques)
tomb figures; 9
Tongzhi, reign; 43, 73-88
Tongzhi, reign marks; 74, 77, 78, 88
translucency (of enamels); 22, 38, 63
Tsui Museaum of Art; 181
turning marks; 17, 58, 75

underglaze blue; 49
underglaze red; 47, 177-217
University Museum and Art Gallery, Hong Kong; 43

van Gellicum; 232
van Oort, H.A.; 72, 108, 148, 151
Victoria and Albert Museum; 108, 178, 212
Vung Tao cargo; 11, 17

Wang Bingrong; 64, 65, 72, 226
Wang Qi; 163
warping; 110
washes, painting in; 14
wear; 81, 116, 181

wedding services; 87, 235
Weishaupt collection; 246
white, glaze; 245
wine cup warmer; 137
Wrightington Adobe Site; 46

Xianfeng, reign; 67-72
Xianfeng, reign marks; 68, 70
Xuande mark; 5, 197
Xuantong, reign; 58, 135-140
Xuantong, reign marks; 135
Xuantong, reign marks (fake); 139, 140

yellow, footrim; 27, 43, 47, 195
yellow, glaze; 9, 20, 56, 57, 78, 104, 106, 136, 157
yellow, ground; 108, 157
Yin and Yang; 32
Yixing, stoneware; 153
Yongzheng, reign; 25-28
Yongzheng, reign marks (fake); 25, 158, 212, 241
Yuan Shikai; 151
yuhuchun ping vase; 199
Yung Cheng; (see Yongzheng)

Zhushan; 165

Find this book on Amazon.com

www.allensantiquesnz.com

Made in the USA
Charleston, SC
12 November 2013